GW00690993

THE CAPTAIN

Tuhin A. Sinha

RUPA
PUBLICATIONS INDIA

Copyright © Tuhin A. Sinha 2012

First published as *22 Yards*, 2008

Published in 2012 by
Rupa Publications India Pvt. Ltd.
7/16, Ansari Road, Daryaganj,
New Delhi 110 002

Sales Centres:
Allahabad Bengaluru Chennai
Hyderabad Jaipur Kathmandu
Kolkata Mumbai

Printed in India by
Nutech Photolithographers
B-240, Okhla Industrial Area, Phase-I,
New Delhi 110 020

To

*Those thousand dark hours in hibernation
that go into making a moment of glory happen*

◆

All those who ever aspired to play cricket for the country

◆

*My parents who have stood by me through
my phases of hibernation*

ACKNOWLEDGEMENTS

This book would not have been possible without the support of a lot many people, to whom I wish to express my heartfelt gratitude. First and foremost, I would like to thank Kapish Mehra for believing in the potential of this most unusual 'cricket thriller'. I shall remain grateful to Nandita Bhardwaj and Nishi Jain for their patience and diligence throughout the editing process.

I wish to thank Aditya S. Chauhan, G. Rajaraman, Khalid Syed, Manish Popat, Mayank Atreya, Raghu Panchmukhi and Ronojoy Chakraborty (in alphabetical order) for helping in research and simply ideating with me on issues dwelt upon in the book.

I am also thankful to my friends – Akshaye Anand, Manasvi Sharma, Madhav Ajgaonkar, Subhalaxmi Ray and Saurabh Vishwakarma – who believed in something rather innovative we did, promoting my first novel. Thanks to their conviction, we could shoot an exclusive promo and music video around the book.

Gratitude is due to all the die-hard Indian cricket fans who have stood by the team through thick and thin and whose zest for the sport continues to grow all the time.

Last but not least, I am thankful to Gautam Padmanabhan and Deepthi Talwar.

THE SQUAD

Asad Iqbal	:	Opener
Amod Roy	:	Opener
Shreyas Mane	:	Middle Order Batsman
Vinay Bhagat	:	Middle Order Batsman
Mayank Pradhan	:	Middle Order Batsman
Jeet Gohil	:	Batting All-rounder
Aslam Khan	:	Wicket-keeper
Ishan Sawant	:	Right Arm Pacer
Baljeet Khurana	:	Leg Spinner
Rajat Shetty	:	Left Arm Pacer
Ramgopal	:	Off-spinner
Naved Khan	:	Bowling All-rounder
Sameer Patel	:	Right Arm Pacer
Rajiv Pandit	:	Middle Order Batsman

1

OLD TRAFFORD, MANCHESTER

22 June 2008

India Beat SA to Enter Twenty20 World Cup Finals

It was a night no true blue Indian cricket fan will forget in a long time. The boys played, and how! The team, after a wobbly start to their innings, eventually edged their way slowly, deliberately, to a nail-biting five-wicket win off the penultimate delivery.

The protagonist of the on-field drama was Jeet Gohil, whose international career was until recently mired in accusations of an 'attitude problem'. At yesterday's match, his aggression anchored India's response with an unbeaten 60 off 45 balls. He ran singles with ease and – as South Africa began to tighten their grip – thumped two sixes off the fifteenth over from Brett Hodge to give his side a fresh lease of life.

Yet, South Africa had their noses in front. India needed 10 off the last over. Aslam Khan flicked the first ball for four past short fine leg; the second ball was a piercing yorker he couldn't do much about, and his attempt to clear the long on boundary had him caught in the deep. The score moved and it came to two runs off two balls. SA skipper Peter Hayden's face looked as lined as the field he was playing on. The dependable Derek Richardson bowled on leg stump, the ball brushed past Gohil's pad and hobbled at an agonisingly slow pace towards fine leg where it just about managed to beat Simon Boje's despairing slide. The Indian supporters, led by spinner Baljeet Khurana, were heading in droves on to the pitch even before the ball hit the boundary marker.

Nothing seemed to work for South Africa in the semi-finals: their batting, with the exception of perhaps George Stevens, lacked fluency; their bowlers were wayward; and their fielders fumbled with overthrows. India, on the other hand, put up an inspired performance, playing like a team possessed. Though the margin of victory was slender, this would definitely rank among the more significant ones for Indian cricket in recent years; certainly, it has come at a much-needed time. Often dubbed 'chokers' and 'paper tigers', India has much more at stake than the Twenty20 World Cup when they take on Australia in the finals two days from now. A win here would be perfect redemption for what happened just eight months ago.

India 139 for 5 (Jeet Gohil 60*, Clive Howe 2-22) off 19.4 overs beat **South Africa** 136 for 9 off 20 overs (George Stevens 35*, Baljeet Khurana 3-20) by five wickets.

◆

LORD'S

23 June 2008

The chill London air has done nothing to dampen the spirits of the boys. They are practising in two separate groups, distributed evenly in two sets of nets. I am facing Ishan, Baljeet and Sameer. In the other net, Vinay is taking guard against Rajat, Ramgopal and Sameer. I am happy at the way I'm middling the ball. My feet are moving just as I want them to; the rhythm seems to be just about perfect.

The tautness in the body language of some of my players reveals their hunger for a major win. And we can't be any closer to that than right now.

The pressure of performing is huge, and justifiably so for a match as crucial as the one we'll be playing less than forty-eight hours from now. There were reports in the media today about a verbal duel that supposedly took place between Amod and our fielding coach Ahmed at the hotel poolside while we were celebrating our victory over South Africa. As per 'reliable sources', the fight allegedly took place because Ahmed had admonished Amod for his poor throwing in the previous match. None of us in the team is even remotely aware of the incident; that the Australian team management planted the report to lower our morale is the obvious inference.

I have no reason to doubt that the final encounter is going to be an intense mind game. The Australians, who have mastered off-the-field antics, are the favourites of the media and sport aficionados alike. I have to admit, I admire the sheer drive they have for victory. But only sometimes. All of us want to win. But would we embrace the same guile to do so? I'm not sure. We play hard, but we play fair.

After a gruelling half-hour session, Amod takes over from me at the nets. I'm pretty satisfied with my batting practice. I've timed the shots well; the foot movement has been good. At the pavilion, I decide to have a quick word with Shiraz Ahmed, who is ready with an intensive fielding practice plan. The thing about the English summer is that it doesn't really get dark before 8 p.m. And since we're keen to practise fielding under the lights, we have more than an hour before we can begin. I am constantly making mental notes and now I wonder whether it will be a good idea to play a hitherto uncapped player in the final. After all, the Australians are sure to have studied videos of our games thoroughly. A spunky all-rounder like Naved Khan could throw them off balance and upset their plans.

As the orange embers of the last rays of sunlight fill the sky, I am struck by the thought that I'm on the precipice of a life-altering moment of history. And I remember another such moment, a moment that altered the cricket in the country; yes, but also set me off on this journey.

It was a glorious day of June in 1983 when eleven men changed the nation's perception of the sport of cricket; when an entire country held its breath while a victory no one had thought possible played out before the collective eyes of the populace.

Back then, we were normally packed off to bed at 9 p.m. sharp. On that night, however, we were allowed to stay up. Three other families had assembled in our house. There was evident excitement in the atmosphere as the adults bustled about, discussing each ball amidst bites of food. Huddled in the midst of this charged ambience, I, along with my friends Montu, Sujit, Rinku, and my brother Tanmay, knew there was something special about this match.

And when India finally won the World Cup that night, pandemonium broke out. Stuffing ourselves into a Fiat and an Ambassador, we drove around the city till about two in the morning. All of Jamshedpur was awake: bursting crackers, exchanging sweets and breaking into impromptu jigs in the middle of the street.

That was the moment that introduced me, first hand, to the kind of excitement the sport generates. That was also the moment when all confusion pertaining to my career miraculously cleared. Mom wanted me to become a doctor; Dad, an engineer; but, as young as five, I knew where my heart lay. And for the next twenty-four years, I dreamt of holding that trophy in my hands.

My parents, though, were difficult to convince. And it didn't help that I let my studies get affected by the practice I was putting in at school. When I barely scraped through to Class 9, my father organised a tutor to come in and teach me Science and Maths every evening.

'Dad, I don't need tuitions. I'm going to study hard this year,' I protested, thinking about all the hours of practice I would lose because of the tutor. Besides, I had just been selected for the Bihar Under-15 team, and there were likely to be matches in the evenings.

'Mayank, you can't depend on a sport to make a living; you need to have an education to fall back on. I think the tutor will really help you focus on your studies.'

And so the argument went on for some time, till I finally said an assertive 'no' to the tuitions. My father and I didn't speak for almost a month after that conversation, until the day when I was batting in one of our key matches and I spotted a familiar face among the spectators. It was my father. He had come to see me bat.

His presence added a zing to my performance. For the first time, I dropped anchor and stood at the crease for all thirty overs of the match. I managed a 78 not out. To top it all, everyone was impressed by my temperament.

Soon there came a point when my parents were no longer ashamed of how I did in school. Montu had gone on to study engineering and Sujit had managed to get into an MBA course; I was bracing myself to represent the country on the cricket field – I had made it to the India A side and done well.

I had fallen in love with the game as a little boy, and that romance had only grown stronger with time. The time and emotion that I had invested in the game seemed to be now reaping rewards.

Fourteen years after India triumphed in the World Cup, I made it to the Indian side.

My debut was at Edgbaston on India's tour of England in the summer of 1997. Strangely enough, playing for the country seemed like some sort of homecoming. I savoured some hostile pace bowling while hitting my first century. But even after having been on the crease for nearly six hours, I felt as fresh as a daisy. What a rush that match gave me!

When I finally returned to the pavilion, a huge chocolate cake sat waiting for me. I cut it in the balcony, much to the delight of the photographers. When I look at those photographs, I see exultation, and also awe, as the sense of the occasion sank in.

How quickly a decade has passed. Today is another English summer; though the occasion, in some ways, is much bigger. Do we have it in us to create history?

'Hey brother, how's it going?' I hear a voice behind me and turn. It's Raghav.

Raghav works with *The Telegraph* and is one of my closest friends. He has stood by me through all the vagaries of my cricketing career. What formed the initial bond, I think, is the fact that we started our careers roughly around the same time. Raghav's first important assignment was the England series of 1997, where I made my debut, and my first interview was with him.

Journalists and celebrities share an oddly symbiotic relationship because a significant chunk of our communication (ironically, even between board officials and team members) happens via the media. And most of us have our own favourite journalists whom we trust and who, over a period of time, even become good friends.

Raghav happens to be a strong votary of the theory that in a match as crucial as the one we're going to play, the team winning the toss should unfailingly opt to bat first, irrespective of the conditions. I tell him about my idea of employing an uncapped player to catch the Aussies unawares, and he thinks it's a good one.

Minutes later, we begin fielding practice. Catching has never been much of a problem with the boys; they have relatively safe hands. The problem lies with their movement. Many of them are slow in picking and throwing the ball, especially when it is on their wrong side (that is, when a left-hander has to pick the ball to his right and vice versa). Most of the boys look pretty agile though, as they go through the drills. I am still concerned about Vinay, Amod and myself. We are all in our thirties and not the quickest on our feet. Hence, I practise separately with them, getting Jeet, our best fielder, to watch us.

Around 10.45 p.m. We are at the dining hall on the seventh floor of the Hotel Intercontinental. The management has acceded to our request and ensured that we have the hall exclusively for our use for an hour. It's important to have the team get some time to bond; hence, on all crucial pre-match days, players are expected to dine together. Our dietician, Mark Stevens, guides each player with a menu that best suits his needs. Within minutes, we're all backslapping and joking. Ahmed and Amod have a hearty laugh together, perhaps laughing at the Australian team management's attempt to create a rift. I chuckle at the thought that their bonding would never stand a chance of making it to the headlines tomorrow.

A special guest who has joined us for dinner is ex-cricketer Vinod Bhargava. As a batsman, Vinod's sheer tenaciousness had made him rise above his average talent. He could stand doggedly for hours against some of the deadliest pace bowlers without really playing any attacking shot, and yet the scoreboard would never stop ticking. Like a workman, he would build his innings with laboriously accumulated singles and twos, totally frustrating the opponents. He was also an effective spinner, mixing both his off-breaks and leg-spins so cleverly that he would often provide the much-needed breakthrough in a Test match.

Vinod retired a couple of years before I started playing for India. In his decade-long career, he was never a permanent member of the side. Rumour had it that he wasn't on the best of terms with the then captain, Jai Prakash, whom he found extremely passive and laidback.

Vinod, however, continued to be passionate about the game long after his retirement. He owned an export business that often required him to travel to the UK and South Africa. And when his trips to these countries coincided with a tournament, he would drop in and mingle with the players. Vinod is known to be an extremely keen observer; in the past, he has pointed out some very minute technical flaws to players. His pep talks have instilled a great deal of confidence in the team.

Earlier in the day, Raghav had told me that Vinod was in London and I had asked him to find out whether Vinod could have dinner with the team. I was told that Vinod would try his best, but he wasn't too sure as he had prior engagements. In the end, Vinod, who is as patriotic as they come, managed to make it.

And here he is at the dining table, once again providing us insights before this crucial match. Vinod, however, isn't too enthusiastic about playing a rookie in the match. It's not that he doubts Naved's calibre, but he is worried about the fact that he would take the place of Ramgopal, who seems out of form. Vinod insists that Ramgopal is too crucial a player to keep on the bench for such an important game. He also thinks we should go with an additional bowler.

Post dinner, I randomly flip through some TV channels. I reach out to the phone to call Revathi, but then realise that it is about four in the morning in India. A few years ago, I would have called her anyway. But then relationships evolve and so do people....

My doorbell rings. I get up with a jerk, nervous that it might be bad news. When I see Raghav standing outside, tension writ all over his face, I know that I'm not going to like what he's about to tell me.

'Praveen Tiwari called up from India. He says he has confirmation from bookies that three of our players have been fixed for the final match,' he announces.

I'm speechless, and a full moment passes as the impact of his words fully sinks in.

'Does he have any idea who these players are?'

'No, not yet.'

I know there is no point questioning Raghav any further. Tiwari is the master of sting operations; he first broke a story on bookies and match-fixing nearly ten years ago, and the reach of his sources remains unparalleled.

Raghav leaves with the comment that, perhaps, the law of averages exists for journalists too, and that Tiwari is wrong this time around. As captain of the side, I can't possibly have the luxury of clinging to that hope. Any trace of sleepiness is gone now. Who could these three players be? I know for sure that the 'genuine match-winners' or 'impact players' are more susceptible to approaches from bookies. I'm also reminded of a whole lot of unpleasant incidents that have occurred with some of my team members in the past, including those that only I am privy to. Based on this, I zero in on five players: Jeet Gohil, Ishan Sawant, Amod Ray, Asad Iqbal and Ramgopal. I know I may be terribly, terribly wrong; I know Tiwari could be wrong; yet this is not a press statement that I'm making. It's a personal assessment based on things I know better than anybody else.

I grow more and more restless with each passing moment. I reach for my laptop and switch it on. Slowly, I click on a file named 'The Captain', and type out the password that is requested. The file opens, and as I begin to read, I realise that I'm trembling. I'm re-visiting a forgotten chapter, one that could complicate my life and my cricket.

✦

2

QUEENS PARK OVAL, PORT OF SPAIN

June 2007

The uncomfortable humidity and overcast sky we all awoke to, that day in Port of Spain, portended the gloom that would come over us by evening, when Ramgopal, India's final wicket, would fall. We were out of the one-day International World Cup, in the very first round. It's difficult to describe how I felt at that point – it was like losing someone very dear, and that too in a freak mishap.

My heart was as heavy as the deliberate pace of our batsmen walking those hundred-odd metres to the pavilion. I cried as I walked off the field; the first time in many, many years. The photographers had a field day capturing my uncharacteristic display of emotions of course; they'd always complained that I was too phlegmatic. And no, contrary to what people said afterwards, I wasn't trying to gain sympathy. I was just a person overcome by a gamut of emotions – feelings that were connected to a trophy I had dreamt about since I was a boy.

I wasn't the only one so deeply affected. Shreyas and Aslam cried too; others such as Jeet, Amol and Vinay were too numb to react. They chose to retire to the familiar confines of the dressing room as soon as they had quietly congratulated the winners.

The next two days were spent in a stupor, with most of us choosing not to leave our hotel rooms. The perpetual media glare did nothing to help the morale of the team. If your body language did not convey abject dejection, it was immediately construed as a sign that your bank balance had been fattened by bookies. So great was the fear of a backlash, that before stepping out of their hotel rooms, a couple of junior players actually dishevelled their hair and moistened their eyes – just for the cameras.

The senior trio – Vinay, Shreyas and Jeet – stayed in their suites for two days, playing cards and listening to music. I too remained indoors for the most part; playing cards though was out of question, as any form of gambling had begun to evoke a certain revulsion in me. For the very first time since I'd taken over as captain, I ignored all calls from the press, even switching off my cell phone. I had nothing to say, and simply wanted to be left alone. News from home filtered through, however. We heard about the mass protests that had begun back home. Asad, who happened to speak to his wife, was told that a *shav yatra* – performed as a part of the last death rites – was taken out in Indore. Eleven people impersonating the team members were carried like dead bodies on people's shoulders, mock funeral pyres were lit and people shaved their heads in accordance with Hindu rituals in the event of the death of a family member. It was crushing to see fans mourn our loss at the World Cup like death. I spoke to Revathi later that night, and she told me of the protests back in Jamshedpur. A small group of people had actually shouted slogans outside my house before the police cordoned off the area.

To be honest, I wasn't really upset about this demonstration of anger from the fans. I've always tried not to get carried away by excessive displays of emotion from fans – whether it's deification in times of victory, or vilification in times of loss. What concerned me was the welfare of our families. As reports kept flowing in, we heard that a cricketer's house had been attacked; yet another uncorroborated report claimed that angry fans had brought down the partly built house of another cricketer. Our own sadness and shame, combined with these incidents, killed all desire to return home.

Two days later, at about three in the morning, a few of us landed at Mumbai; those from the north had flown to Delhi. Apprehension gnawed at our insides as we stepped into the airport. What kind of reception awaited us outside? Our nervousness was not unjustified: we were told that around five hundred people had assembled outside, waiting to greet us with garlands made out of slippers. Fortunately, the Indian Cricket Board (ICB) had coordinated with the airport authorities so we could leave through a rear exit. My old friend Raghav was the solitary figure waiting there to receive me. We took the earliest flight out from Mumbai to Kolkata where my father and wife were waiting for me. I looked at my father, trying to decipher his feelings. He smiled at me and, reaching out, hugged me warmly. I felt relief at the show of support. It meant more than anything else to me.

We drove down to Jamshedpur, escorted by a gun-toting policeman that the government had provided for my safety.

As I entered my house, a strained silence greeted me. My mother ushered me in with a forced smile, which made me feel worse. As we sat down for dinner, we tried making small talk, but the effort was eventually too much and slowly each of us lapsed into silence.

Later that night, my father came to where I was sitting, pretending to read a book. 'I understand what you're going through, Mayank.

But now it's over. Treat it like a bad dream and start thinking about the future.'

I shook my head, 'It's not that easy, Dad. Apart from how I'm feeling, I have to formally talk to the media soon. I have to communicate with all those people we've let down.'

Sleep eluded me that night, as images of other press conferences, other captains handling difficult situations, flooded my mind.

The next morning, camera bulbs flashing in my face, news cameras pointing at me, I took full responsibility for the showing. 'Yes, we batted, bowled and fielded poorly. We didn't apply ourselves at all. But ultimately, the responsibility lies with the captain, and I take complete responsibility for how we played.'

Expectedly, someone asked about my rift with Dave Symonds, and I, expectedly, dismissed the allegations.

Suddenly, a journalist called out from behind, 'How do you feel being responsible for the death of ten people in the country?'

I froze. 'Sorry?'

'Well, yes,' the journalist continued, 'those are the figures that we currently have with us. Three fans and four bookies, it is reported, have committed suicide, and three people had fatal heart attacks after India's defeat.'

I couldn't speak for a minute. I looked around at the crowd of faces gazing at me expectantly. Finally, I said, 'I apologise to all my countrymen for letting them down. I'm very, very sorry.'

I stood up and walked away, ignoring the hundred questions being shouted at my back.

When I reached home, news channels were beaming the interview on repeat. Dad walked up to me and patted me on my back, 'You're very brave.'

Just at that moment, my cell phone rang. It was the ICB president, Sunil Kapoor. 'I need a detailed report explaining the reasons for India's poor performance,' he said without preliminaries. 'It needs to be exhaustive. All those responsible for this shame should be exposed and booked.'

'Yes, sir.'

'We've fixed up a Special Action Committee, and the first meeting is scheduled on next Monday. You can present the report there, personally.'

His harsh tone stayed in my mind long after I had hung up. I started thinking about the report he wanted me to write. I knew if I set about telling the truth, few people would get a clean chit. And yet, I knew in my heart that the clean-up process had to start at some point. Regardless of what it might mean for the careers of some of the country's most adulated cricketers.

✦

3

SABINA PARK, KINGSTON

10 June 2007

Kenya Trounce India

Kingston: At times, playing against an unheralded side is more perilous than playing a better matched rival. One, not having played much against the weaker side, you are unaware of their real strengths and two, with the odds stacked in your favour, you are inclined to take them for granted.

This complacence, however, cost India dear as Kenya pulled off a shock win against them in the humid atmosphere of the jam-packed Sabina Park at Kingston. After putting up a respectable 242, Kenya bowled India out for 214 to score a neat 28 run win, thereby inflicting a major blow to India's World Cup campaign. Kenya was truly the deserving winners, first amassing 242 after having been reduced to 94 for 5 at one stage, and then supporting it with some inspired, outstanding fielding and bowling.

Indian captain, Mayank Pradhan, won the toss and put Kenya in to bat. For Kenya, it looked like an old story as their top order once again wastefully gave away their wickets leaving the team in doldrums. Ishan Sawant and Rajat Shetty had both the openers dismissed in the first five overs. Soon after, Dilip Shah was run out stealing a single that simply wasn't there and Frank Ongondo was out stumped by a very neat piece of work from Aslam Khan. At one stage, it seemed the side would be bowled out for under 150. However, that was not to be. For Kenya, the hero was truly 21-year-old Oris Odoyo. Playing only his fourth match, he piled up a mature 72, cobbling up some valuable partnerships in the middle. Odoyo displayed exemplary temperament in pacing his innings, not going for the slog till the very end. In the odd circumstances, Odoyo's innings could well be considered a masterpiece and gave sufficient indication of his future utility for the team. Inspired by Odoyo's effort, the tail-enders too chipped in handsomely, with Kenneth Obanda striking a brisk 31 off 20 balls. Obanda later followed up his cameo with the bat, with some astute bowling which the Indian batsmen found hard to negotiate.

The Indian chase started on a rather shaky note. Amod was out third ball of the innings, beaten all ends up and his middle-stump dislodged. A while later, just when it seemed like Asad and Vinay had settled down at the crease, Thomas Tikolo lapped up a difficult catch at point to dismiss Vinay. Later, when captain Mayank Pradhan and Aslam Khan were putting together a threatening partnership, spinner Bob Ouma struck by dismissing Aslam, getting him caught by Odoyo at mid-wicket (160 for 6). Obanda then returned for a third spell in the final overs, dismissing Rajat and bringing his team even closer to victory. Mayank's presence at the crease, though, still kept the odds tilted in India's favour. The deteriorating pitch, however, did little to help India's cause as the ball kept low for most part of their innings. And when a direct throw by Dilip Shah from mid-wicket had Mayank stranded way out of his

crease (170 for 7), the outcome was pretty much apparent. A valiant
29 not out by Baljeet in the closing stages did excite the crowd but
remained inconsequential. And no sooner was last man Ishan dismissed
than a pall of gloom descended upon the entire stadium.

India couldn't have asked for a more dampening start to their World
Cup campaign, losing to minnows Kenya. Indeed, they needed to do a
lot of introspection and find out if the analysts had erred in pitching
them as one of the favourites to win the World Cup.

Kenya 242 for 8 off fifty overs (Oris Odoyo 72) beat **India**
214 all out off 48.3 overs (Asad Iqbal 63, Mayank Pradhan 50) by
28 runs.

✦

The first week of the World Cup dealt us a nasty double whammy:
first, Kenya defeated us, making all our calculations go awry. And
then, when we had barely regained our balance from the shock
of defeat, news trickled in that our pacer Ishan Sawant had been
charged with doping by the World Cricket Council and had been
pulled out of the team.

Nishant Javdekar, Director Operations, ICB, was making an
announcement when we switched on the television. Apparently, the
board, as signatory to the WCC's Anti-Doping Rules, had carried
out dope tests on the squad a month ago, the first time ever in the
history of Indian cricket. The results were sent to the nearest World
Anti-Doping Agency laboratory, in Malaysia, for analysis. 'They
told us one sample was positive – that of Ishan Sawant – and the
chairman was duly informed,' Javdekar said.

The decision to recall Ishan pre-empted the embarrassment of
him being found guilty during the tournament. The WCC had,

according to the ICB, been informed of the situation. And we would now have to do without our main strike bowler.

The development left the team and the fans shell-shocked. Not so much me, though, because I knew what perhaps no one else knew.

◆

4

WANKHEDE, MUMBAI

2001

It was about seven years before this episode that I had first met Ishan. We were scheduled to play a Test in Mumbai, and I had asked for additional rookie pacers to bowl for me during net practice at the Wankhede Stadium. I thought their full-blooded pace bowling would prepare me for the upcoming tour of Australia starting later that month.

For the next two days, I batted for four hours every day, negotiating their rising deliveries and sweating to regain my lost form. Most of these pacers, who were still in their teens, were fairly unimpressive, except for one. A lanky eighteen-year-old, Ishan, gawky, with unkempt hair, caught my attention. He bowled at an incredible pace, and though he knew little about swinging the ball, he had two potent weapons that he would use alternately to devastating effect. The first was his almost perfect yorker; the second was a sudden rising delivery where the ball virtually jumped onto the batsman's face from a good length area. I was actually hit twice by Ishan's rising deliveries, and a bruise I sustained on my finger kept me out of action for a week.

I made some enquiries about Ishan; a school dropout, he had been staying with a friend at a tenement in Mahim for nearly three years. This made me a little curious, since my source also mentioned that his relatives lived only a few hundred metres away. He had a rebellious streak, I could see that; and his inexplicable bursts of rage on the field had rendered him into a sort of loner. What intrigued me was his attitude. There was an aloofness in his demeanour, a certain fearless devil-may-care attitude. He didn't care what the world thought of him and, strangely enough, that had already made him a winner of sorts.

I recommended him strongly for selection to the BRE Pace Foundation in Bangalore, and within a couple of months, Ishan was training under the legendary Geoff Wiley. Wiley taught him the nuances of swing, and with swing added to his deadly pace, Ishan became a more formidable bowler than ever. The next year, he made his way into the Ranji team for Mumbai. With an impressive thirty-two wickets under his belt in his debut season, and a couple of disciplinary reprimands, Ishan broke into the Indian side. He was then twenty.

He debuted against the Lankans. Though he didn't quite make wickets tumble in that series, his arrival was registered. At a consistent pace of 145 km, a near bodyline length and bounce, he was hostility personified. Amod, who was then the vice-captain and would soon go on to become the captain, shared my conviction in Ishan's abilities. Moreover, Ishan had the right aggression – both in terms of body language and his acerbic tongue. I heaved a big sigh of relief: finally we had a pace bowler who could intimidate. So far, our pacers could only impress.

I was proud of Ishan, and he, in turn, always gave me credit in interviews. Ishan and I shared a protégé-mentor relationship. While Ishan had a gang of his own within the team that he would hang out with while on tours, he maintained a respectful distance with me.

In no time, he went on to become one of the leading bowlers in world cricket, invariably occupying a place among the top five in WCC cricket rankings. His late reverse swing, at an awesome pace exceeding 140 kilometres, made batsmen nervous. Even the likes of Marsh and Richards made sure they came to face him with the added protection of a chest and elbow guard, as his bouncers were difficult to get away from; besides, he would bowl beamers far too frequently, though he would instantly tender an apology.

Meanwhile, off the field, his lifestyle became increasingly wild. This, combined with his aggressive bowling, meant that he was soon embroiled in one controversy or the other. In fact, he seemed to have an inescapable knack for courting controversy. The first, of course, was the one in which he was accused of chucking; an accusation that almost killed his career.

✦

5

December 2004

We were touring Australia when it happened. It was the first day of the third Test match. Already a comfortable 1-0 ahead in the series, the Australians were reduced to 35 for 4, thanks to Ishan's impenetrable bowling. The Perth wicket is perhaps the bounciest in the world, and there is a particular trick by which a bowler can exploit the wind to his advantage. Ishan had discovered this trick from his interaction with an Indian cricketer who played club cricket in the city and the result was deadly. Ishan had scalped both openers in his fiery first spell; even the Aussie captain had a tough time negotiating him and was lucky to survive two close LBW appeals.

Suddenly the West Indian umpire, Gordon Patterson, infamous for some of his rather unreasonable decisions against teams from the Indian subcontinent, gestured to me, indicating he wanted to speak to me. I walked up to him, assuming that this had to do with sledging. After all, our close-in fielders, this time around, had been especially instructed to reciprocate all the (un)pleasantries they received with equal gusto. Instead, to my astonishment, it was to inform me that he was reporting Ishan for throwing. I was dumbstruck. Yes, Ishan was known to bowl certain deliveries where his arm wouldn't quite come from over the shoulder. But to suggest that he 'chucked', was indeed a grave charge.

I remembered what I had recently read somewhere: 'If you want to crush a pace bowler, tell him his bowling action is actually a throw. Being a chucker is the ultimate cricketing humiliation, bringing into question the player's skill, his honesty and his commitment.' How true, I said to myself as the words continued to ring in my mind. Ishan was not allowed to bowl for the rest of the match. Later, we were informed that his action would need to be cleared by the WCC before he could play again. Those were tough days for Ishan and for the team. The transformation in Ishan was shocking. His confidence seemed decimated, and he was only a shadow of his former fierce self.

As per WCC norms, Ishan was to go to Melbourne to have his bowling action tested by biomechanics experts. If they found that he was, in fact, throwing, he would have had to alter his action significantly. Altering a set bowling action, unlearning everything and settling into a new rhythm is no mean feat for a sportsman. You might as well pronounce a death knell for his career.

I could sense Ishan's anxiety. A loner from the start, he now completely avoided all of us, spending his time alone, brooding in his room or practising in the field.

Ishan finally left for Melbourne where the University of Western Australia and the Hong Kong University of Science and Technology analysed his bowling action. Photographs were taken at a thousand frames per second from six different angles. Barring just six out of the over hundred deliveries that Ishan was made to bowl, his action was deemed to be perfectly normal. The report concluded that the 'throwing' was a mere optical illusion and that his bowling action was perfectly legal. Ishan did have a slight deformity around the elbow area because of which he was unable to straighten his arm in those deliveries where the effort to generate more pace would impose a strain on the elbow. Thus, the committee concluded that it may just appear as though he is bending his limb when in fact he's not. His action was, therefore, deemed legal.

Soon after, during a Test match that we were playing against the visiting Pakistani side, I had to sit out due to a sprained ankle. It was a strange experience for me; to watch an international game sitting in the pavilion. I decided to utilise the opportunity to study Ishan's bowling action.

And what I saw left me flabbergasted. Ishan's deliveries followed a pattern; there was one ball every over where his arm would not come over his shoulder – a dubious usage of the elbow was apparent. What was more striking was that the other five balls of the over were bowled normally. I watched Ishan closely in all the twelve overs he bowled, and the pattern remained consistent. The flawed delivery could be any ball of the over and Ishan mixed up the balls pretty well in very interesting permutations and combinations. The flawed delivery was bowled at a speed of at least fifteen kilometre per hour above his normal speed and came back in sharply in a late reverse swing. With his bowling action now cleared, I realised, it had become easier for Ishan to get away with it.

That night I went to meet Ishan in his room. He was playing a video game that had by then become his favourite pastime on most tours. He particularly enjoyed playing baseball. He said he picked up tips from the virtual bowlers in the game. He was surprised to see me at that hour. We soon got down to chatting over a drink.

'I quite admire your genius, beta,' I said out of the blue.

Ishan looked confused.

'You chuck quite intelligently now. Nobody even suspects you anymore.'

I had caught him completely unawares. He looked at me nervously, and began, fumbling, to say something. I reached out and patted him on his shoulder, cutting him off: 'Mind you, a thief is not a thief until he is caught.'

He smiled at me, relief apparent on his face.

My reasoning was simple. The definition of fair and foul, in most cases, is purely subjective. If the WCC felt so strongly about the occasionally erroneous bowling action of a pacer, who after all did genuinely suffer from a minor deformity, by what logic did it remain silent about something like sledging, which, at times, takes place at every ball of the match? Why did it not initiate action against umpires who, despite the availability of technology, jump to hasty decisions and often give a batsman caught behind when television replays clearly show a different picture? And why did the WCC allow batsmen to call for runners, even when it was abundantly clear that the batsman wasn't really injured and that the move was a ploy to distract the fielders?

The fact is, morality, as in all other aspects of our lives, has become equally subjective in cricket too. Hence, that night, I was in no way critical of what Ishan was doing, though, as I walked back to my room, I did wonder whether I had done the right thing. But, of late, I had also begun to wonder if there was any such thing as absolutely right. I guess I was getting conditioned to believe that everything was right, until labelled wrong. So, I let the matter rest. We won the series 2-1; and with Ishan taking eighteen wickets, I saw no reason to alter my decision.

6

TRENT BRIDGE, NOTTINGHAM

June 2005

The next time Ishan found himself in the midst of a controversy, we were in England. A tour in that country is always special as the weather throughout the season is ideal for swinging conditions. Our first Test had been at Lord's, and we had won that quite handsomely, with Ishan bowling match-winning figures of 10-134 in the match.

Lord's in London, along with the Melbourne Cricket Ground and the Eden Gardens in Kolkata, indisputably ranks among the most historically significant cricket grounds in the world. Playing in any of these fields motivates you more than usual, because performing well at any of these venues adds a shine to your career's moments of achievements. Besides, I've always been particularly fond of Lord's because it was on this ground that India won the World Cup.

One of the ground's defining characteristics is the significant slope across the field. The north-west side of the playing surface is some eight feet higher than the south-east side. This slope causes appreciable deviation in the bounce of the ball on the pitch, making it easier to move the ball in to right-handed batsmen when bowling from the Pavilion End, and easier to move it away when bowling from the Nursery End.

We had left the Lord's grounds with the English team very disgruntled. When our second pacer Rajat came to the crease to bat, he was greeted with a couple of jellybeans at the crease. The connotation was obvious: Rajat had managed a huge deal of swing in the English innings, and the English players had assumed that it must have been the result of applying sticky jellybeans to the ball. In another situation, such a far-fetched assumption would have been treated with the disdain it deserved, but I felt that the WCC tended to give a sympathetic hearing to 'white' teams, and hence, even allegations as wild as these were taken seriously. However, the matter lost momentum beyond a verbal altercation between Rajat and the irascible wicketkeeper, Joe Smith.

The real problem arose during the second Test at Trent Bridge in Nottingham, when television cameras caught Ishan scratching the ball with his nails. He did plead later that he was only removing grass that had stuck to the ball, but it was of no avail. The footage caught on the camera was enough evidence of ball tampering. After the day's play, I was called, along with Ishan, for a hearing with the match referee.

Before the appointed meeting with the match referee, I took Ishan aside. 'Did you actually do it intentionally?' I asked him upfront.

After the chucking episode, our mutual trust had only grown and I was quite confident that Ishan would tell me the truth. Ishan nodded. He did look remorseful. I'm not sure whether the remorse was because he'd betrayed my faith or because he felt guilty about breaching the laws of the game.

I wasn't shocked, because I was reaching a stage where nothing about Ishan shocked me anymore. 'Then say as much to the match referee. There's no point saying you were removing grass because the video tells a different story.'

Dave, our coach, and the team manager had a different opinion: they felt Ishan needed to deny all allegations, and stick with the story that he was trying to remove grass. They had spoken to the ICB president, they said, and he was prepared to spin the story so it would appear as if WCC was only acting out of disgruntlement with the ICB.

Just as we were walking into the match referee's cabin, the manager whispered, 'I hope you have understood what you have to say. This has been decided after consulting the ICB president; we have to stick to it.'

Hence, reluctantly, I accepted the diktat. As expected, the match referee did not buy the denial and Ishan was fined seventy-five per cent of his match fee and suspended for two matches.

By the time the hearing was over, it was very late. The team had already been sent back to the hotel and the two of us, along with Dave, were to head back together. Before we left for the hotel, Ishan and I took a walk around the ground. We were pensive. There was a lot to talk about, and yet we didn't know where to begin. We walked to the centre of the ground – that stretch of twenty two yards through which the ball travels to meet the bat. And then I simply turned towards Ishan and looked into his eyes. He knew that I wanted an answer.

'Bhai, everybody does it. Everybody,' he tried to defend himself.

'Look Ishan, that doesn't absolve you. When did you start doing this?'

Ishan had the grace to look embarrassed. 'Bhai, as you know, I played for Surrey for a couple of months last year,' he said. 'During a league match with Lancashire, I came across the Pakistani cricketer, Junaid Kamal, who was playing for them. Junaid was the leading wicket-taker that season, remember? His reverse swing was the topic of conversation at all the county clubs. We hit it off well; every night we'd go out to some nightclub or the other. One night, we both got quite drunk, and in that state, he started blurting out some … some things.'

'What things?' I prompted, because he'd paused, as if unsure whether to carry on.

'He said that ball tampering had been going on for a really long time, even in the seventies and eighties. Apparently, the Pakistani legend, Yusuf Iqbal, was an old hand at it. For years, he didn't share his secret with anybody, but just before he retired, he passed on the trick to a couple of the younger guys. Had it not been for TV cameras catching bowlers at it in the nineties, it would probably have gone unnoticed.'

'So did Kamal teach you how to tamper?' I asked, shocked at the seeming omnipresence of the practice.

'Yes. I'd met this woman, a bartender, and had gone out with her a couple of times. Kamal had the hots for her, but she wouldn't pay him any attention; she called him "the horny Paki". Kamal finally begged me to set him up with Demi.'

'And you did?'

'Yes, for a price. I asked him to tell me everything he knew about ball tampering.'

'Bloody pimp,' I mumbled, torn between disgust and admiration. On the one hand, it reflected Ishan's shrewdness in acquiring ammunition that made his bowling more lethal, and, on the other, it was just another indication of the levels of corruption that had seeped into the supposed 'gentleman's game'. This lad was way beyond my comprehension in an interesting yet intriguing way.

As is well known, bowlers shine one side of a new cricketing ball while the opposite side is left to deteriorate through natural wear and tear. This helps bowlers swing the ball in the air – the shiny side travels faster through the air, while the rough side acts as a brake, pushing the ball in the direction of the rough side. But as the ball loses its early shine, it begins to swing less and it is not until it gets older and rougher that it begins to deviate again, a process known as reverse swing. This process is precipitated by artificially roughening the surface. At times, this has been done using finger nails; at other times, by scratching the ball with, say, a bottle lid. Cynics have even suspected the application of jelly beans and chewing gum on the ball to cause swing.

This then, I surmised, was the mystery behind the powerful reverse swing that some of the world's most renowned pacers managed with an old ball. Despite the obvious immorality of tampering, I was suitably impressed with how these bowlers – many of them college dropouts – had used the laws of science to their advantage.

And yet, a part of me would have none of it. I remembered another peculiar instance of ball tampering that had created news in recent times. It involved our very own Shreyas Mane. Shreyas was caught on camera sticking a portion of some sweet onto the ball, which, it was alleged, would help the reverse swing.

While Shreyas himself insisted that the action was accidental, arguing that the lozenge fell from his mouth, the match referee seemed convinced that the act was deliberate.

Personally, I was quite surprised that a senior cricketer of the side could be so irresponsible – the recent controversies involving ball tampering ought to have made him more careful, I thought. Knowing Shreyas, I could say with certainty that he was innocent. Fact, however, remains that his intentions notwithstanding, he did violate the rules of the game. And a crime shall remain so, no matter how innocently it is committed.

The act merited punishment and it was duly delivered – a fine of fifty per cent of the match fee and a one-match suspension.

Ishan interrupted my thoughts to say that he knew of at least two promising cricketers playing first class cricket for Ranji teams in India, who regularly indulged in the practice. Perhaps they could afford to do so because most domestic matches are still not captured on camera. Then, as if still trying to defend what he'd done, he said, with a fair degree of surety, 'Bhai, at least, one out of every three pacers in the world has indulged in ball tampering at some point of time or the other.'

From what Ishan told me, and from whatever instances of ball tampering – whether proven or alleged – had surfaced during my playing career, I knew one thing for sure: it was a far more layered issue than we thought. Neither could it be swept away under the carpet with any degree of ease. In fact, it must have been the omnipresence of the practice that led the coach of a leading international side to suggest that ball tampering be legalised.

On the surface, the suggestion seemed absurd and irresponsible. But when I dwelt on it, I realised that it was indicative of a desperation, the significance of which could not be ignored. Let me explain: I quite agree with those who believe that the game in its modern format is loaded heavily in favour of batsmen. With the dominance of one day cricket and the advent of Twenty20 matches, bowlers are being reduced to whipping boys. And logically, as in society so in cricket, inequality does lead people to hit back and flout some rules. I guess the bowlers were determined to hit back now, and this was their chosen path to make their presence felt.

Despite all the rationalising, the issue caused me considerable distress and sleepless nights. I did empathise with the bowlers' predicament in a game that is obviously inclined in favour of the batsmen. No batsman's batting stance has ever been questioned. Batsmen haven't been barred from moving about in the crease even as a bowler takes his run-up. Nor has a batsman ever been restricted from keeping a high back lift, instead of having the bat grounded at the crease at the time of delivery. In fact, there is no conventional batting action or way of holding the bat. And let me emphasise here that I'm not condoning illegal bowling. What I seek to emphasise is that the rules are far more lenient for batsmen who get away with things as against a bowler who has to conform to numerous and varied strictures.

I strongly believe there hasn't been a bigger disservice to the game than the infamous incident in 1981 involving Greg Chappell. Playing against New Zealand, with one ball left and six runs to be made, Greg had asked the bowler (his brother, Trevor Chappell) to bowl underarm, that is, to roll the ball along the ground so that New Zealand batsman Brian McKechnie would not be able to score a six to tie the match.

It caused a furore. The then New Zealand Prime Minister termed it a disgusting incident; his Australian counterpart seconded him; the act, he said, was contrary to the spirit of the game. And underarm bowling was subsequently banned. I endorse this; it is, I think, this kind of act that should invoke the most stringent punishment, and not something like a minor deviation in the movement of a bowling arm, which is difficult to establish even after a thorough evaluation.

Even after all that, cricket rules are still more lenient for batsmen. Take for instance, how, in 1979, Dennis Lillee, also Australian, actually batted with an aluminium bat and got away with only a reprimand.

Australia were playing England, and were in trouble at the end of the first day, at a score of 232 for 8 with Lillee not out. When the second day of play began, Lillee emerged on the field carrying a cricket bat made from aluminium. The bat, manufactured by a firm of Lillee's good friend Graham Monoghan, was intended as a cheap replacement for schools and developing countries. Nevertheless, Lillee decided to use it in the Test as a marketing stunt, and at that point, there were no rules against using such a bat. This was not the first time Lillee had used an aluminium bat: he had employed one twelve days previously in a Test against the West Indies, without incident.

The trouble began on the fourth ball of the day, when Lillee pulled up a straight drive on a ball from Ian Botham. The ball went for three runs. However, Australian captain Greg Chappell thought it should have gone for a four, and instructed someone to give Lillee a conventional willow bat. As this was happening, English captain Mike Brearley complained to the umpires that the metallic bat was damaging the soft leather cricket ball.

Although the umpires told Lillee to change his bat, the batsman announced that he wouldn't and positioned himself to face the next delivery. Brearley, Lillee and the umpires held an animated discussion for almost ten minutes, before Chappell decided that the game would be held up if things continued. He walked into the ground, took one of the willow bats from Hogg, and instructed Lillee to be quiet and use the bat. Lillee threw away his aluminium bat in disgust, and grudgingly took the wooden bat.

Shockingly, Lillee was not disciplined for the incident. Both the umpires and the Australian Cricket Board decided to let Lillee off with only a warning. And Lillee's attempt to market the bat worked: after the game, sales of the bat skyrocketed for a few months, with Monoghan giving Lillee a small cut of the profits.

It was after this incident that the laws of cricket were amended to specify that the blade of the bat had to be made of wood.

The next morning before we took to the field, I called a meeting of all players and addressed them collectively.

'What is legally wrong cannot be justified by making it an emotive issue of nationality or colour. It is a fact that Ishan did indulge in ball tampering; whether it was done consciously or whether he was genuinely removing grass is something he knows best. But henceforth, if any one of us indulges in an act that goes against the rules and spirit of the game, I'm not going to stand by him. So, all of you must read the WCC clauses. Ask me if you don't understand anything. We'll play hard, but we'll play fair.'

More than the players, what I said was meant to be a clear message to the coach and manager as well. Because I knew that the manager, given his proximity to the ICB's chief, would tell him about my outburst as soon as he could. And frankly, I wasn't bothered. I knew that shielding my team from corrupt and negative influences of any kind was going to be an important challenge for me if I had to produce the results I aspired for. And it didn't matter to me even if the corruption had the backing, direct or tacit, of people in positions of influence.

My outburst was obviously communicated to the ICB president, Kapoor. And to my pleasant surprise, he supported my no-nonsense attitude. I, too, realised that he was not such an awful character after all, but politics is such a double-edged sword that once you are in the thick of things, you have to be a part of it; or rather, it is a part of you forever. I also came to the conclusion that more often than not, politicians knew what was right, even if they espoused the wrong causes. After all, all of us do things that best serve our purpose. Ishan, too, was doing precisely that.

I must confess here that Ishan's chucking and ball tampering offences hadn't quite prepared me for the bigger magnitudes that his problems would escalate to. Drug abuse, after all, to the best of my understanding, did not serve him any purpose.

✦

7

BARBADOS

13 June 2007

Three days had gone by since our defeat at the hands of Kenya and we had one day to go before our next match against Zimbabwe in Barbados.

Under normal circumstances, a victory over Zimbabwe would have been a foregone conclusion; but things were different this time round. Even the bookies were taking no risks. Normally, the odds for an Indian win would have been 20 paise against 120 paise. This time it was 60 paise against 120 paise. We were upset at the way people were talking about the team, and this strengthened our resolve to score a huge win and redeem ourselves.

On Sunday, a day before the match, I decided to allow myself the concession of sleeping a bit beyond the time I usually get up, but that was not meant to be. At around 7.45 a.m., I was woken up by the ringing of my doorbell. Annoyed that someone had paid no attention to the do-not-disturb sign on my door, I decided to ignore the bell. But when it rang a second time, I reluctantly got up and answered it. It was Shinde, our team manager, and the grave expression on his face betrayed the unpleasantness of the news he bore. What had happened was that two of our players, Baljeet and Rajat, had almost drowned while partying on a boat at Accra Beach on the South Coast the previous night. They were both drunk when the incident happened, and had only been saved by the quick thinking of a more sober person on the boat.

Both Baljeet and Rajat were too shaken to practise that day. I was livid, but their presence in the team for the all-important game against Zimbabwe was crucial, especially after Ishan's exit. Therefore, Dave and I chose not to reprimand them. In any case, we felt it had been our own fault for not setting up stricter codes of conduct for the tournament. While the players were required to be back in their rooms by 10 p.m. on the night preceding a match, there were no such rules for the other days. Ideally, the players should have had enough commitment to draw those lines themselves; unfortunately, that rarely happened.

What made matters worse, was that the episode quite expectedly generated a lot of negative publicity for the team, with media back home picking up the story. A small consolation was that the media was not fully aware of all the details of the incident. While Baljeet and Rajat were reported to have gone for a swim, and lost control after much partying, the truth was that the two had been trying to pick up two Brazilian women who were playing hard to get. Baljeet and Rajat followed them from a pub in downtown Barbados to the beach. Apparently, they also partied a bit on a boat. It was perhaps the result of the excitement that Rajat, who was sloshed, lost control and fell into the sea. The same fate nearly befell Baljeet who tried to save him. It required some deft and timely action by the boatman to save them. The two women, apparently, also duped them of a good amount of money.

I was appalled at the way two adult men, representing their country, had been swayed by lust. But when I thought about it, I realised that I had forgotten the impact women have had on our cricketing fortunes over the years.

◆

8

REVATHI

How a woman's presence imparts that special something to a man's life dawned on me when Revathi became a part of my life. When I think of her contribution in the way my life has shaped up, it makes me realise just how lucky I've been.

I was barely a couple of years old in international cricket when I was locked in a major dispute with my celebrity agent. Thanks to my naiveté, I had been signed on a five-year contract for an amount far below my market worth. While there was a clear clause that stated that the amount would be revised at the end of each year, the agents conveniently overlooked it. I retaliated by signing a sponsor on my own accord. My agents, thereafter, threatened to file a suit against me. It was at this messy juncture that I was introduced to Revathi, who was the daughter of a family friend. She had recently qualified as a lawyer and was an intern with her father, who happened to be a leading lawyer in Jamshedpur. It was to seek a legal opinion that we had approached Revathi's father. And since her father was out of town that day, Revathi attended to me in his absence.

After just moments into a conversation with her, I was convinced that I wanted to hire her as my lawyer. This surprised many people, including her, since she had just started practising. In hindsight, I don't know whether it was my knack for backing dark horses (like I'd done with Ishan), or whether it was her clarity of thought, or her personality, or all of these. But I decided to go with her. She travelled to Mumbai to fight my case, and eventually had it poised in my favour, leaving my agent no choice but to call for a compromise after agreeing to all my conditions.

That court battle proved to be our courtship. We never really went out on dates, or had conversations like I imagine people do when involved in a relationship. Being an international cricketer, one seldom gets time for this. Instead, in a year or so, while the case was going on, from being a novice in cricket, Revathi went on to become one of the most ardent followers of the game. She would surprise me with her observations. For instance, when I had a bad series in Sri Lanka, she actually pinpointed a technical flaw that had crept into my game without my realising it. The surfeit of one-dayers had made me play across rather than straight even in Test matches, and that had become my undoing, so I was getting bowled out to pacers. Similarly, I became more aware about legal matters and started following her cases.

Soon, a time came when the need for conversation became insatiable, and that is when we decided to bridge the gap and get together. We got married within one-and-a-half years of our first meeting. And ever since, Revathi has been my support system.

While I feel lucky to have Revathi in my life, my heart goes out to all those cricketers whose personal problems have adversely affected their performances on the field. The absence of an emotional anchor often creates its own set of problems.

Principally speaking, what a cricketer does in his personal life is none of my business. It should not bother me whether a cricketer is happy to be in love with one woman or whether he enjoys dating several partners or whether he has no interest in women at all. These are entirely the cricketer's prerogative.

However, an obsession with women can become a major setback for a cricketer's career. I know of cricketers, either married or committed, who habitually indulge in flings. They do it for the 'kick'. They see a one-night stand as some form of a quick-fix healing therapy that de-stresses them and induces an impassioned performance in the next match. And being an international cricketer offers you innumerable opportunities for 'flings'. Some cricketers even see it as a necessity – or as a perk of the job.

Whether these flings actually lead to an impassioned performance will be evident if an investigation is carried on the activities of the said cricketers in the forty-eight hours leading up to the start of play.

One such cricketer who believes in this 'therapy' is my much-married friend, opener and ex-captain Amod. We made it to the Indian team almost at the same time. In fact, he arrived with a bang and achieved success much before I did. I did catch up with him soon though. Having started off together, we shared an unspoken though healthy rivalry. Or at least everybody around us assumed we did. Soon after making it to the Indian team, Amod was acknowledged by, the people who matter as being 'captain material', and within a year, he rose meteorically to the position of vice-captain. However, his subsequent inconsistency and indiscipline cost him dear. He never quite lived up to the promise he showed in his first year.

A year after making it to the Indian team, Amod married his girlfriend, Kritika, who he had been dating since his college days. They made a striking couple, and the media flashed their pictures all over the news channels.

However, something somewhere went wrong soon enough. Amod, by nature, is a restless character; he gets bored of things pretty fast. I can't say whether he got bored of his wife or of marriage, but he never appeared very enthusiastic about his personal life. The disillusionment, in fact, could be seen in his game too. The fire in the belly seemed to have been extinguished.

He began cheating on his wife occasionally, and then on every tour abroad. He just had to spot a sexy woman in the disco or in the hotel pool, and he would go right ahead and make a pass at her. Four out of five times, the girl wouldn't refuse – such is the charm of international recognition. I suppose it has to do with the demigod status that being an international cricketer catapults you to. A fellow cricketer, whom I played with in the Ranji Trophy and who couldn't make it to the national side, once said, 'There's no abode on earth better than a 70mm cinema screen and the cricket field. Once you are there in the middle, you are god, and everyone who watches you, deifies you.'

This has its flip side, of course. I know of some cricket colleagues who were dumped by their model/actress girlfriends the moment they were ousted from the team.

Amod justified these flings by viewing them as essential stress busters on high-pressure tours. We once discussed his behaviour at length over a drink. Needless to say, he was high, and therefore, possibly more open than he would have been otherwise.

'So you don't feel any guilt pangs about these flings?'

'Why? Why should I?'

'You and Kritika had a 'love marriage'; you've known each other since college!'

'We got married seven years ago. You think in today's age, where everything moves so fast, a marriage will last seven years?'

I looked at him and said yes, I was pretty certain it should.

He shrugged and said, 'Well, Kritika and I realised soon after marriage that certain relationships work only till the point they are not bound in marriage.'

'But what really went wrong?' I asked out of curiosity.

'Everything, I guess. Kritika says I'm too self-obsessed. She says I can't think beyond my game, my training and my endorsements.'

I nodded; it was a predicament all of us faced.

'I mean,' Amod was saying, 'in the short career that we have in international cricket, we live like vagabonds most of the time. There are such huge expectations to perform, to just retain our places in the side. And then when we get the little bit of time in between, we need to sign up as many endorsements as we can.'

There is no denying that international cricket does take a heavy toll on our personal lives. I've invariably felt guilty for not giving Revathi the attention she deserves. She never complains, though. On the contrary, she has sacrificed a great deal, especially as regards her own career. I remember once we were on a gruelling eighty-two day tour of Australia. Revathi could not travel with me as she had some important hearings interspersed over those months. However, it was a phone conversation that I had with her, after a big defeat at Melbourne, that made her virtually abandon her professional responsibilities back home. I must have sounded terribly depressed; it also happened to be Christmas Eve and being away from family on festive occasions makes the loneliness that much more unbearable. In just three days, Revathi was by my side at Sydney. Her presence marked a turnaround in my performance. I loved Revathi for this.

For some other cricketers, it's different. The physical presence of their wives makes no difference to them either on the field, or off it. I remember an instance when a senior cricketer was with a prostitute in his hotel room in Cape Town when his wife, along with the wives of two other cricketers, had gone for a day tour of a nearby mountain.

'Does Kritika have any idea about your flings?' I asked him.

'I guess she has her suspicions. After all, she knows about Tarana.'

Oh yes, how could I have forgotten Tarana. About four years ago, Amod had met Tarana, a well-known television actress, at a party. He had immediately fallen for her, and when she had reciprocated, there was little he could do to stop himself from succumbing to the temptation. They had an affair that went on for some six months. While the media flashed their pictures together, both maintained that they were just 'good friends'. The affair ended when Kritika supposedly stumbled across some strong evidence that Amod could not deny.

There was another side to the Tarana-Amod affair. Around the same time that Tarana entered Amod's life, his on-field performances became rather erratic. And on a couple of occasions, his concentration seemed so impaired that he gifted his wicket away just when he seemed to have settled at the crease. It was quite logical to attribute it to the effect of the personal dilemmas he must have been facing at the time.

And the story had another angle to it as well – something that largely remained unconfirmed. Raghav – my usual source in these matters – was the one to tell me about the rumours that Tarana had been planted in Amod's life by Barry Chauhan, the underworld don who had set up a huge empire in Hong Kong. Usually referred to as just 'B', Chauhan was said to control virtually eighty per cent of the cricket betting business.

'It must have been traumatic for Kritika, when she discovered your affair,' I continued.

'Yes, I guess.'

'Didn't she want to leave you? How did you convince her not to?'

'I guess she didn't have much option. I mean, she would have been the loser had she left me. Could she find a richer, more popular husband? Besides, there is a way to win back your wife once you've been caught with your pants down.'

'And what is that?'

'Cry in front of her. Tell her it's the first time you've strayed. Blame it on everybody and everything else – the circumstances, the girl, your friends and so on. Act the victim and then take her on all the tours for the next few months. Once she begins trusting you again, you can start taking some liberties.'

I was quite shocked to hear this. One, because I never quite saw the same shrewd planning going into Amod's game. And two, a person who cheats on his wife is likely to cheat others too.

'You're quite experienced in handling extramarital flings,' I said.

Missing the sarcasm, Amod smiled and said, 'Credit goes to Vinay. He told me about these tricks.'

I smiled at the thought of someone else hearing what Amod had just said. Vinay has an image of being incapable of doing anything wrong. Such is his status amongst cricket lovers that any hint of an allegation against him runs the risk of being considered blasphemy. But, of course, reality was far, far different.

With an impressive aggregate of over seven thousand Test runs, ten thousand one-day runs, and an immaculate, technically flawless batting style, fans revered Vinay. And his image was untarnished. In a career spanning over twelve years, he had not been involved in a single controversy. The truth was that Vinay too was a philanderer, though his modus operandi was different. Or rather, more sophisticated. He had a girlfriend each in at least five different places around the world. In India, his rendezvous would take place in Kolkata and

Bangalore. He liked to talk about them as his 'good friends' to those who knew about them.

Now Vinay presented such a guile-free persona that nobody could, even in their wildest imagination, think, even for a second, that he was having multiple affairs with these women. He presented a near perfect picture of being a good husband and doting father. And yet, the fact remains that Vinay was always involved with at least half a dozen women at a time.

Once, talking about the strange relationship Vinay and Sonam, his wife, shared, Raghav had said, 'Look, it's quite obvious what happened. Vinay meets this rich guy's daughter at a Page 3 party and instantly falls for her. Once they get married, however – and they did within three months of meeting – they realise that they belong to different cultures altogether. Coming from a conservative background, Vinay never quite approved of Sonam's relationship with her male friends.'

'So how come he's started a business with one of her male friends?'

'Who? Atul? Well, he came to Vinay with the business proposal. He wanted to set up a chain of power gyms, using Vinay's name. And since the proposal already had Sonam's endorsement, Vinay could do little but agree.'

'Oh, so that's how Vinay Gym and Fitness started.'

'Yeah, but Sonam's proximity to Atul soon began annoying Vinay; that's what led to problems between the couple.'

'So were Sonam and Atul actually having an affair?'

Raghav laughed aloud, 'Who knows? These things are best known only to the two persons involved.'

'So do you think Vinay started having affairs to get back at her?' I asked.

Raghav laughed again, 'Well, it's like the chicken and eggs story. I don't know who strayed first, but yes, they currently have an understanding between them – each is allowed to do what he or she wants.'

There are some men who brag about the number of women they have slept with. They do this to the extent that it almost seems as if they need some reassurance about their masculinity. I'm not sure whether such behaviour can be attributed to a form of low self-esteem, because I'm sure Vinay and Amod can't be classed in that category.

The thing about Amod is that he is someone, I sense, who is bitter – both professionally as well as in his personal life. Unlike Ishan, he is not impulsive. My reckoning is that he has probably clearly worked out in his mind how he is going to behave with each player. For instance, he is either extremely friendly or patronising towards people depending on what he thinks he can get out of them. I think it was this attitude that cost him his captaincy. There were accusations of camp formations, which I would objectively hold to be true.

Also true – and this worries me particularly – are the accusations of selfishness on the field. People suspected that he purposely slowed down his scoring as he approached his hundred; this despite the fact that the team's required run rate continued to mount. But would he be so selfish as to put the country's hopes for the T20 World Cup at stake? I hope not.

✦

9

AUCKLAND, NZ

February 2003

Vinay and Amod were not isolated cases. I knew that several other cricketers, whether single or not, seemed to have no control when it came to women. Two of them left the team before I was inducted. One of them, a middle order bat, had set up a strange barter system with an actor friend. The cricketer would woo a woman, promise her marriage, and then, after a month, say it wasn't working out and that they were better off as friends. He would then set up this girl with the actor friend who, in turn, would set him up with another girl. The practice went on for quite sometime, till the cricketer's skewed priorities got the better of his game and he was reduced to acting in nondescript TV serials.

The other cricketer – a left arm spinner – had an unfailing tendency of falling for his teammates' girlfriends. He would watch out for phases when a teammate and his girlfriend would hit rough weather in their relationship. Chivalrously, he would offer the girl his shoulder to cry on, listen to her, support her completely, share romantic poetry, and then propose to her. He is said to have employed this technique twice in the Indian team and once in his Ranji team. The results were disastrous in all cases. Ultimately, this behaviour found him being accused of creating a rift between team members, and apparently became one of the contributing factors for his ouster from the team.

The cricket team invariably has at least three eligible bachelors at any point in time. They are normally the ones who are known to hang out in groups and frequent discos and pubs when we tour abroad. Baljeet, our leg spinner, is one of the most talented bowlers in the world. A tall and well-built 'cut surd', he is one of the more popular bachelors on the team. However, he is also a chauvinist, who likes adding to the count of women whom he has got lucky with on each tour. Five years ago, he had announced his arrival on the international scene with an impressive eighteen-wicket haul against the touring Englishmen. However, on the tour which succeeded that, I discovered a bizarre side to him.

The first Test at Christchurch in New Zealand had been washed out in the incessant rain and we lost the second at Wellington, which put us under a great deal of pressure before the final Test at Auckland. Anxiety kept the much-needed good night's sleep at bay on the eve of the match. I awoke early and decided to step out for a walk to refresh myself. As I was crossing across the hotel reception, I was shocked to find one of the new players of our squad, Sankalp, sleeping on a sofa in the reception lobby.

I woke up Sankalp to find out what the matter was. Initially, he was reluctant to talk, but I pressed him and he revealed what had happened. Apparently, his roommate, Baljeet, had brought a girl into the room at around two in the morning. Baljeet had woken Sankalp up, and asked him to leave the room.

'And you did what he asked?' I said in shock.

Sankalp didn't say anything, but I understood; our bench strength in those days was known to be bossed over by the seniors.

'But where did he get this girl from at two in the morning? Was she a call girl?'

'No, it's Eliza, the correspondent who has been covering these matches for that New Zealand TV channel.'

I knew who Eliza was. An overly flirtatious young correspondent, who didn't hesitate to give a warm and close hug to a sweaty cricketer after a good performance.

Later that morning, our then captain Sharad lost the toss and we fielded first. Baljeet looked weary, and was unusually lacklustre. He sent down 14 overs for 62 runs without any wickets.

That evening, I walked into Baljeet's room. He instantly saw that I wasn't in the best of moods. 'What happened? You seem tense, Mayank bhai,' he said.

'Your performance was pretty mediocre today,' I remarked.

'Yes, bhai, I just couldn't get into my rhythm,' he said, sounding apologetic.

I must admit here that most members of our side have been respectful towards their seniors even when they've had a man-to-man talk like the one I'd initiated with Baljeet. I came to the point right away.

'How will you get into your rhythm unless you sleep well before the match?'

Baljeet was taken aback when he heard this.

'How's Eliza in bed?' I asked. 'Good?'

Baljeet was ashen faced. For a few moments, he fumbled for words. Then he said, 'Bhai, I'm really, really sorry. For god's sake, don't tell anyone.'

'Anyone else knowing about it is really not that important as long as you realise what you've done. I mean, is this your sense of responsibility towards your country?'

Baljeet looked down, apparently in shame.

'You know this was a do-or-die match for us, yet, instead of focussing on the match, you were doing something else.'

'Bhai, I just don't know why I couldn't control myself. I'm so sorry. I promise I will never do anything like this again.'

I decided not to report him to the team management; at times, one needs to live up to the expectations of trust the other person shows in you, even at the cost of ignoring rules. I trusted Baljeet and believed he wouldn't make the mistake again. Unfortunately, the damage had already been done, and we lost the Test match despite Baljeet's fine bowling in the second innings. Since that day, however, Baljeet has never given me reason to complain. He is still into women big time, but now he knows where to draw the line.

✦

10

KENSINGTON OVAL, BRIDGETOWN

15 June 2007

India Beat Zimbabwe

Bridgetown: After the beating India took at Kingston, they seemed to have come into this match determined to redeem themselves. And they did it in great style.

The architects of this victory were Vinay Bhagat, who hadn't been in great form lately and rookie Rajiv Pandit, who was inducted at the last minute due to Shreyas' injury. Together they put up an astonishing display of aggressive batting – perhaps the best that you could ever get to see. Indeed, so dominating were they that the Zimbabwe team remained mute spectators throughout. The pair put up a partnership of 300 plus and after reaching their individual centuries, both the batsmen broke into virtual carnage. Surprisingly, Rajiv was the faster of the two, scoring 22 in one over from Eddo Sibanda that included two fours and two sixes. He eventually got out to a mistimed shot to mid-wicket.

At the other end, Bhagat continued the assault. He improvised with great finesse and amazing power. Young bowlers like Sibanda tried to stick it in the black-hole, but Bhagat quickly got his left leg away and kept smashing to and over mid-wicket. He even smashed four full tosses thrown by the bowler to four different corners of the field. All records were shattered as Vinay and Rajiv registered the highest partnership in one-day cricket.

The Zimbabweans came in to bat with a daunting asking rate of nearly 8 runs an over, which looked improbable right from the start. Skipper Pradhan placed his men intelligently, giving away the singles but blocking the boundaries. And it worked just the way it was meant to – the batsmen soon got frustrated and started gifting away their wickets. Tom Taibu mis-hit to mid-on, Heath Masakadza was out LBW, plumb in front of the wicket, Captain David Brent was stumped out when he stepped out to hit Baljeet. Grant Taylor was out caught in the deep. Tito Price was run out. The match was over long before closing time.

This thumping victory was just what the Indians wanted to keep their morale up for the remaining matches and with that performance, they sure deserved it.

India 382 for 4 (Rajiv Pandit 184, Vinay Bhagat 155*) off fifty overs beat **Zimbabwe** 210 all out in 39.1 overs (Oris Odumbe 47; Baljeet Khurana 3 for 28).

✦

The victory against Zimbabwe was an emphatic one; exactly what the team needed. And of course, rookie Rajiv's showing was brilliant. Rajiv was a last-minute inclusion because Shreyas had woken up that morning with a high fever.

In only his fifth ODI, Rajiv had scored what could well be his career's highest ODI score. That it came about in a high-pressure match (regardless of who the opponent was) and off 150 balls, surely spoke of the promise of this cricketer.

The victory came as a big morale booster for us. It put us in a positive frame of mind for the next match against West Indies. Things did not seem as bleak as they did before the game against Zimbabwe.

We had four days to go before the next match. And I would have liked all my cricketers to isolate themselves and concentrate on mentally preparing themselves for it. However, that was not to be. For two days after the match, Rajiv was locked in negotiating deals with three of the country's top celebrity management firms who had their people stationed in the Windies, ready with lucrative contracts.

It was ironical: just twenty-four hours ago, this guy had not been sure of his place in the side; and here he was all set to enter the world of 'controlled corporate cricket'. Bhagat's stars were also shining: his contract with a soft drink major had been extended by two years. And a confectionery manufacturer had mooted the idea of shooting an ad with Rajiv and Bhagat together. Plenty of rewards were already being heaped on our cricketers in response to their impressive showing against Zimbabwe, when our future at the World Cup was still so precariously perched.

Few would dispute the fact that one of the biggest problems that plagues Indian cricket is money. Before 1983, it was the dearth of it, post that it has been the surfeit.

Nothing can possibly prepare you for the overnight fame that being part of the Indian cricket team accords you. And when you've graduated to this level from life in a smaller town, it is just that much more difficult to come to terms with.

Over the years, there has been a change in pattern: Mumbai, which once happened to be the Mecca of Indian cricket, now has just two cricketers playing for India; Delhi has just one. And six of our regular cricketers in the side, and that includes me, come from the smaller towns. Asad Iqbal is from the outskirts of Indore; Jeet Gohil is from Baroda; Aslam Khan is from Etawah; Ramgopal is from Trichy, and the pacer Rakesh is from Raigad.

Asad had to travel thirty-five kilometres and change two buses to reach the cricket stadium. Aslam had to give up the comforts of home to shift to a sports hostel in Lucknow at the age of thirteen. Sameer learnt pace bowling just by observing Javagal Srinath and Venkatesh Prasad on television. After he missed out on a junior level district trial due to illness, his uncle brought him to Pune. They knocked the doors of several clubs, till a coach finally noticed Sameer's talent and he was inducted into one of the club teams. Ramgopal had to quit his engineering studies at the end of the second year as better cricketing prospects required him to shift to Chennai. It must have been an extremely tough decision, as he had stood third in college. But then, life is all about choices and he was brave enough to make a difficult, not to say risk laden, choice.

As for me, I belonged to the sleepy steel town of Jamshedpur. But compared to these other cricketers, I guess I was fortunate to have faced lesser difficulties. My routine, though mostly during my high school days at Loyola School, was no less rigorous: up at 6 a.m., off to school at 7; classes would commence at 7.40 a.m. and get over at 1.15 p.m. Cricket practice would take place between 3 and 5.30 pm.

Those staying close to the school could go home after school and return for practice after a quick bite. But since Telco Colony, where my family then lived, was nearly twelve kilometres away, I had to kill nearly two hours all by myself. It was a lonely two hours. The same place that seemed so vibrant and full of energy when classes were on, would suddenly seem haunted. I would search out some isolated corner, have my lunch and desperately wait for it to be 3 o'clock.

In the evenings, I had to change two mini buses to get back home and by the time I reached, it was 7 p.m. and I would be exhausted. When my father finally began to see prospects for me in cricket, he turned quite supportive. He built a net with a concrete wicket in our backyard and installed lights so that I could put in an additional hour of practice at night, under his watchful eyes. He would throw the ball at me for a full hour although he couldn't roll his arm over to bowl; Dad, though passionate about the game, had never played the sport himself. And that was not surprising. Cricket before 1983, was a big-city game.

So one can understand that fame and wealth affects these boys. And the wealth is astounding: as per the most recent contract we signed with ICB, players in Grade A are to get ₹60 lakh per year; those in Grade B ₹40 lakh; Grade C ₹25 lakh and Grade D 15 lakh.

Besides the annual contractual payment, players also receive fees for the matches they actually play. The match fees are ₹2,50,000 for a Test and ₹1,50,000 for an ODI.

But, of course, the money earned from playing only constitutes a fraction of a cricketer's earnings. The major bucks, for most of them, lie elsewhere.

In the team, Vinay is clearly way ahead of others when it comes to earnings from endorsements. After him, there's Amod, me and Jeet. We can draw anywhere between one and a half to three crores for a yearly contract for a single brand. Even the younger players, by virtue of a couple of good performances, manage something like fifty lakh for a contract.

And that wasn't all. About five of our cricketers had contracts to write columns for newspapers. I found this a bit amusing, because at least two of these cricketers hardly spoke in important team meetings. I wondered if, as a strategy, they saved their ideas for their columns. The prevailing rates for these articles were quite lucrative – approximately sixty thousand rupees per article.

And then, three of us – Vinay, Amod and I – had a contract with a news channel each for an exclusive five-minute chat at the end of the day's play. These quick chats would bring in anywhere between sixty lakhs to 1.2 crores annually for us.

Now this kind of money could easily turn someone's head, let alone someone who has had to struggle to make ends meet. I've heard of instances when players have feigned injuries in order to fulfil a commitment to a sponsor. It was Raghav who told me that our former captain Amod, who had pulled out of a Test match against Sri Lanka three years ago on the pretext of a hamstring injury, was actually secretly shooting for a television commercial. Apparently, the company had threatened to sue him as Amod had not been able to give them the contracted number of days for the last two years.

There have been other instances when cricketers have skipped parts of preparatory camps or turned up later than scheduled, before the start of a Test match. I had pulled up Baljeet for this once. Baljeet had been candid: 'I was shooting, Mayank. It's the first time I've been asked to do a music video.'

'Were you the one singing?'

'No, but the singer is a childhood friend so I couldn't say no.'

Annoyed, I had barked, 'Why don't you take the match off and promote his album?'

Sometimes, these endorsements had a more direct effect on our games. For instance, I was told that Shreyas, who sported the logo of an electronics goods brand on his bat, was told that the amount he would be paid for each match would be directly proportionate to the time he occupied the crease. So, Shreyas would come in – he played at number three in ODIs – with the main aim of occupying the crease as long as he could, even to the detriment of the team's score. It worked occasionally when we batted first, especially in some difficult conditions in England, New Zealand or Australia, but more often than not, his slow pace did us in. It was difficult to say anything to Shreyas because of the clout he enjoyed as a senior player. So we had to move him down to bat at number five. That worked: the number five batting position in ODIs is a position that doesn't allow you too much breathing space. You've got to immediately get on with things or else you'll be blamed if something goes wrong. Though Shreyas protested initially, once the team management put its foot down, he had to go along with the decision. Shreyas did accelerate the scoring in his new position, though this meant that he sometimes wasn't on the crease for as long as he probably would've wanted. The result was that the logo soon disappeared from his bat. Apparently, the sponsors were unhappy and did not extend the contract.

Then, there was another clause that certain brands made their endorsers sign. It stated that, if a cricketer had to sit out for five consecutive matches, then his deal amount would be reviewed and cut by a certain percentage. Hence, when Amod was the captain, he ensured that none of his favourites sat out for five consecutive matches. He would make sure they played at least one match in between, to ensure that their deals were not revised. Expectedly, this eventually led to the formation of cartels that prevented newer players from breaking into the side.

One of the more serious stories I heard, was how two big brands had actually bribed a couple of selectors to keep Jeet in the side, despite his rather reckless showing for the past six months. I was part of that selection committee meeting when two selectors firmly put their foot down and insisted that Jeet remain in the team. Their reasoning was that Jeet, being an 'impact' player, could turn the match around anytime. My reasoning was that, if an impact player comes good in one or two out of ten matches, then we are taking a big gamble by including him in the side for the remaining eight matches.

Sometimes, with the hectic pace at which cricket is played these days, the best thing to happen to a player not performing for a prolonged period is to be kept out of the side. The schedule of international cricket today is so demanding, one simply can't work on one's flaws while the season is on. Many times, a break has worked wonders for players when they've actually gone back, played domestic cricket, rectified their flaws and bounced back stronger. I wished Jeet had done the same. Instead, his sponsor friends paid some ten lakhs each to two of the selectors. For the company, those twenty lakhs would have been a very small amount compared to the losses they would have had to suffer in the case of Jeet's omission; but for our selectors, it was a lot of money. In their view, perhaps, compromising the team's interest was a very small price that they were prepared to pay to earn this reward.

✦

11

ASAD IQBAL

The pressures of international cricket can be relentless and can show up in multiple forms. Everybody, from your fans to sponsors and journalists, wants to have a piece of you. And then you are grappling with all the mundane engagements which sometimes make it so difficult for you to remain focussed on your cricket. The sudden transition doesn't affect just the cricketer, but also his family, resulting in situations one could never have imagined. Take for instance, what happened with Asad once.

Asad's father owned an eatery located on the highway connecting Indore and Bhopal. Once, a blistering century by Asad against Pakistan had the entire Indore-Bhopal highway blocked for over two hours. A whole barrage of journalists converged upon his father's dhaba to record his reaction; other travellers stopped by to catch a glimpse of what was happening. And soon enough, there was a traffic jam that took over two hours to clear. Subsequently, Asad's father, Mohammad Iqbal, kept his dhaba shut whenever Asad played an ODI.

Asad's rise to international cricket makes a great inspirational story. As I've mentioned before, Asad travelled thirty-five kilometres and changed two buses to reach the cricket stadium. His parents never understood their son's interest in the game: they had never even seen a cricket match being played. Asad had an elder brother, Mohsin, whom he was very close to, and two younger sisters, Alvira and Aqeela. The only person who supported Asad's pursuit of cricket was a maternal uncle, Wajid, who stayed in the main city. In fact, it was Wajid who got Asad admitted to a school which offered cricket-coaching facilities.

When Asad failed his Class 8 exams, his father made him quit cricket and study in a school that was closer to home. The travelling time saved thus, was expected to be spent in helping his father at the dhaba. Asad hated it. Two months later, he left home. Wajid stood by Asad and let him stay with his family. Asad's estrangement from his father made him all the more determined to prove his mettle in the game. And when, two years later, Asad became the youngest player to make it to the Madhya Pradesh Under-19 side, his father realised that, perhaps, he was wrong. Tragedy struck then: Asad's brother, Mohsin, died in a freak mishap on the highway. His death affected Asad so much, that for a year thereafter, he could barely concentrate on cricket. Asad once told me that, whenever he faced a ball in those days, images of his brother would haunt him and he would end up playing a reckless shot. It took a long while before Wajid motivated him to get back to his game, telling him that Mohsin, wherever he was, would be terribly unhappy if Asad stopped giving the game his all.

Nearly five years later, Asad got a break in the Indian side. He came in with a reputation of being one of the biggest hitters in domestic cricket. Asad was selected for our tour of New Zealand that winter. Amod's injury during the one-day series made me a little adventurous and I asked Asad to open the batting. What I got from Asad would have done any captain proud – a 72-ball 105 in windy conditions at Wellington. The left-hander's innings comprised four sixes and eleven fours. Asad was soon being compared to Sri Lankan prodigy Jayadharan, who had earned a reputation for ripping apart the best bowling attacks in the world.

In no time, Asad came to be considered a match winner. Vinay Bhagat may have scored the most number of runs and centuries in our team, but in every crunch situation, he has failed. Asad, on the contrary, thrives under pressure, and his performance goes up a few notches just when needed.

For two years, Asad was consistently good. He scored five Test centuries and six in ODIs. After Srikant, he was the fastest opener we had. The problem started in my first series as captain – the home series against England. Something was terribly amiss with Asad; I was unable to place my finger on it. He seemed to be a mere shadow of his former self. He was unusually tentative in his stroke play, while his feet movement was non-existent. In five Test innings, he aggregated just 43 runs with a top score of 20. Gone were the dashing square cuts and the elegant on-drives. He didn't seem to even spot the bouncers right – the same bouncers that he would hook over the boundary so effortlessly.

I noticed that he would take unusually long walks at the crease before each delivery; after getting beaten, the first thing he would do was pretend that there was some movement on the sight screen that did him in.

I did have a pep talk with Asad before the third Test. The result was no different. He only put himself under greater pressure by curbing all his natural strokes and trying desperately to just stay at the crease.

Finally, after the match, he came to me. 'Bhai, I'm sorry. I'm under a lot of tension.'

'But why?'

'I don't know ... I just feel so afraid.'

'Afraid?'

'Yes, afraid that I'll never be able to achieve the big scores that I've got so far. That I'll never be able to play my best shots again.'

Asad told me that he had been experiencing a sleep disorder as well. Sometimes, he would stay awake till two in the morning, even on match days; he was always short on sleep.

I had a long chat with him that day. I thought Asad's was a classic case of burn-out. I advised him to opt out of the ODI series against England and take a break. I reasoned with him that this break would recharge and relax him. Asad, however, was worried that he would lose his place on the side. On his insistence, he played the first three matches, scoring 34, 0 and 0. I finally persuaded him to sit out of the last two matches. I also spoke to a leading psychologist, Parsekar, in Mumbai, and fixed up Asad's meeting with him.

Counselling did help Asad to an extent. He came back into the side for a triangular tournament in Sharjah. In all the four matches that we played, Asad hit some blistering strokes that were reminiscent of his past flamboyance; yet in all the four matches, he floundered and gifted his wicket away just when he seemed set for a big score. His highest was a measly 36.

Later that year, Asad's anxiety problems seemed to have only compounded. In a most crucial Test series against Australia at home, he was all but a bundle of nerves. Television cameras actually caught him trembling before each delivery. I knew something was terribly wrong. One evening, I spotted Asad sitting alone in a corner of the dining hall. The place was empty as it was still early evening. I went to Asad and patted him on his shoulder. He turned around, almost scared.

'What's the matter, brother?' I asked him reassuringly.

Within moments, Asad was baring his soul. Perhaps, what he had been going through had just become too much for him to bear alone.

'In January this year, just before the England tour, I got a short break of five days and decided to spend it with my parents in Indore. One night, much after midnight, four people arrived at our place in a jeep. They forced their way into our house. They told my parents not to worry, that they were servants of god and just wanted to speak to me in private. Three of them then forcibly entered my room, and one remained on vigil outside. They were carrying a laptop and one of them, who called himself Hamid, played a CD on it. To my horror, the CD had terrible images of rioting and arson in Baroda. There were heart-wrenching images of abandoned children, and people pleading and begging for mercy even as they were being butchered.

'"This is the country you are representing," they kept saying. "It has given us nothing except suffering."

'I still had no idea what these men wanted me to do. Hamid then explained: "We are leaving this CD with you. Watch it again and again till your blood boils. And if this doesn't happen, then trust me, you don't have blood in your veins, only water."

'The second person, called Anees, was more direct. He told me, "The day after tomorrow, you are supposed to get the Arjuna Award from the president. Go and throw it back on the old man's face and hand this CD over to him. Tell him we don't need these token gifts."

'After they left, my father told the local police about what had happened. Realising the sensitivity of the issue and also unsure about the culprits' connections, Abba had requested the administration to keep the matter confidential, which they did. The result was that two constables were deployed outside our house. Abba told me not to think about these men and that I should feel proud of getting the award. I did go accept the award, but those images stayed in my mind, and haven't ceased to haunt me since. There were so many questions on my mind, and I had no idea who I could talk to. Every time I face a bowler, blurred, gory images from the CD crowd my mind. I can't concentrate. I can't take this anymore, bhai. I just can't take it anymore. I'm finished because of this CD. My game, my career is virtually over. Tell me what to do.'

Asad broke down and I spontaneously hugged him.

What Asad blurted out had left me confounded. I waited for him to calm down before asking him what was worrying me.

'But do you believe what those four men told you?'

'What?'

'That this country has given your community nothing except suffering?'

'Of course not, Mayank bhai,' he shot back. 'Nobody can question my family's loyalty, or mine, towards my country. My grandfather was a freedom fighter. My father went to jail during Emergency. And yet the images of the CD were such that they just don't cease to haunt me. I am helpless.'

I thought about the problem for weeks. It baffled me more than any other problem had, simply because of the complex emotions involved. I spoke to Parsekar again, telling him the whole story, and then Parsekar, Asad and I sat together for a session. I tried to talk to Asad as much as possible; my underlying objective was to make sure he was in a positive frame of mind and that the demons inside his mind had been exorcised.

By the time the World Cup had come around, Asad seemed to have struck his old touch again, but I couldn't be sure.

24 June, 2008

It's 7.20 a.m. As I think of Asad's peculiar story, I think about the psychological strain of being trapped in 'another world' and how disturbing it can be, especially when one has to face the constant pressure of expectations. I have come across people like him who have lost it mid-way, because their success has alienated them from the people they grew up with. Guilt and loneliness, or both, tend to make people impressionable and more susceptible to manipulation. And when the manipulation is laced with religious sentiments, it is all the more potent.

Asad is possibly the most crucial member of our ODI side. If he stays at the crease for twenty overs, even the Australians know how difficult it is to keep us from scoring more than three hundred. With the strong middle order that we have, a big total is ensured and a win is all the more likely. That is the sole reason we made an exception with Asad and kept him in the team although he was not in form.

Yes, logically, Asad probably stands a very good chance of being approached by bookies simply because of the impact his style has on the game. But I know how emotional and sensitive he is. And emotional guys are largely emotional *for* a cause that they have chosen; not against a cause.

I don't think Asad would ever indulge in 'fixing'. If I know him well enough, he's the sort of guy who would probably beat up a bookie if one dared make such an offer to him.

To be honest though, I think I have been dwelling on these players to avoid getting back to Ishan's incomplete story – a story that still haunts me, the way it did when I first heard it.

✦

12

CHAK DE!

It is 7.40 a.m. and I'm too exhausted to read any further. I haven't moved any further in figuring out who the three men might be, who the bookies have paid off. This means I will now have to play the most important finals of my life with the knowledge that our team will only have eight members. And these eight will be competing with fourteen opponents: three faceless ones from our side.

I recall that I am carrying with me a DVD that a TV commentator friend of mine had assembled especially for me. This DVD has highlights from some of the most glorious moments of Indian cricket: India's 2-0 Test series win against England in 1986; a couple of exciting India-Pakistan matches including the 1985 Benson & Hedges World Championship final where we beat Pakistan by eight wickets. Matches that show that games are won or lost in the mind.

My mood changes considerably as I watch the DVD. For all the suspicions I have about some of my team members, I can't help remembering moments when they had done the country proud.

Vinay had once batted with an excruciating back pain against the West Indies side, way back in 2000, to help us win a crucial match, where we had our backs pushed against the wall for most part of the game. In the process, Vinay risked aggravating an injury that could have been detrimental for his career. Vinay's discomfiture was apparent when he batted; every few overs, he was treated with ice cubes. Yet, his willpower kept him going, and in the end, we won the match with just two wickets remaining. The innings, though, aggravated his back problem and Vinay had to sit out for the next six months.

Baljeet once bowled a full spell with a fractured jaw against the Australians. Despite being hit while he was batting in the second innings, he went on with the bowling with his face plastered. After the game was over, the entire audience at the Sydney Cricket Ground stood up and gave Baljeet a standing ovation.

I remember the time when Shreyas was rushed to hospital because he was dehydrated after hitting a century in unusually humid conditions in the Port of Spain on the third day of a Test match. He was discharged in a few hours, but was advised not to take the field the next day. Despite this, Shreyas fielded in the last session on the fourth day, just to make sure that he spent the required amount of time on the field to be allowed to bat in the fourth innings. And then on the fifth day, he occupied the crease again for fifty overs to help us win the match.

This was the same Shreyas who was so keen to keep an endorsement that he had even sacrificed his team's interests to stay at the crease for as long as he could.

As captain of the team, Amod had gone into the final Test of a series in South Africa when his father was being operated for a heart bypass surgery back home. Amod had been given the option of returning, but he didn't. We were one down in the series, and the sheer desire to try and win the last match to level the series had Amod stay back and fight it out.

Amod's attitude had earned him immense respect from everyone in the cricketing fraternity. Another instance when Amod's actions had earned admiration was when he was dropped from the side two years ago. Well-wishers had advised him to hang up his boots, as his chances of getting back into the side appeared bleak. Instead, he overcame the odds and fought back, playing local-level cricket during off season, for which he even travelled to far off playing centres in Himachal and Haryana.

I wonder how the same Amod could have faked injuries and, at one point, given unnecessary leeway to some of his favoured players which led to indiscipline and factions in the team.

I remember another instance when Jeet had batted with a sprained elbow, as it was a crucial triangular series match against New Zealand. He smashed six copybook ground strokes to hit six boundaries in the over. And this was in the tenth over when the Power Play was in force; that too in chilly, breezy conditions at Wellington. How I wished such quality performances became a rule rather than the exception for Jeet.

Thinking of these brighter moments makes me feel a bit better. I get up and look out of the window. It is drizzling. I go back to my bed, lie down, and fall asleep.

Three hours later, my phone rings; it's Raghav. He wants to come over and talk.

In another half hour, we're deliberating on the same issue. Raghav has spoken to Tiwari again, but Tiwari had no further leads on who the bookies have bought. I wonder if it's a good idea to inform the WCC Anti-Corruption Unit. Neither Raghav nor I am reluctant: we're both hoping that Tiwari has got the wrong information this time.

We decide on a plan of action: I'll speak to Dave about the information; depending on how he reacts, we might talk to our senior-most and most trustworthy player, Vinay. Together, we could keep a tab on all our players and devise a fresh code of conduct for the next two days. And that might include banning the use of cellphones altogether.

It's 1 p.m. and I'm at the dining hall. We're supposed to leave for practice at 2 p.m., so everyone is having a light lunch. I tell Dave that I need to have a word with him. We move away with our plates and occupy a corner table, overlooking the beautiful and serene pool.

'I've been told that three of our players have been fixed to under-perform tomorrow,' I say.

Dave, to my surprise, doesn't look too shocked. He asks me for my source of information. I tell him about Tiwari's call to Raghav. He smiles, somewhat wryly.

'You have no proof, do you?'

I shake my head.

'Then forget about it and concentrate on the game. Or else, you'll be opening a Pandora's box for nothing,' he says matter-of-factly.

I'm surprised at his phlegmatic reaction.

He continues, 'It's probably just a rumour. The WCC's Anti-Corruption Cell is too powerful to allow any of this nonsense. So, chill.'

I decide not to pursue the subject with Dave. I never quite liked him. Also, though he was recommended by a couple of our top ex-players, including Vinod, I never quite found him as involved as he ought to have been.

By now, it's 2 p.m., and everyone is ready to leave for practice. I'm tired; I take some hot lemon tea to kill the overwhelming desire for sleep.

13

It's 3:30 p.m. at Lord's. After about half an hour of warm-up exercises, we begin with a rugby session. The idea behind this is to focus on mental conditioning and agility before we begin with the actual cricket practice. Most of the players do take part in the rugby game, though it's not mandatory. Some back out of it for lack of skill. I normally like playing rugby, but I know that today it's important for me to conserve my energy. After all, practice has just begun and my energy levels are already down.

I sit by the border of the playing field, observing the boys as they pass the ball around. I know I need to talk to Vinay, but don't feel like pulling him out of the match: his passion, even while playing rugby, lifts my spirits. Aslam is the fastest; he is the team's guru at rugby and lives up to his reputation today. Amod is clumsy, but then fitness was never his forte. Asad seems a little depressed. I'm not sure what the reason might be. Jeet is in top form – aggression personified. But there is something wrong with Ishan. He looks almost as lost as he did in the days after he was accused of chucking in Australia. I step up my scrutiny. He looks anxiously towards one of the empty stands, and then to the other far end of the ground. He seems restless. Could he be one of the people the bookies have bought?

I walk to the pavilion. As I drink another cup of lemon tea, I think about Ishan.

I had felt confident that, with the chucking and ball tampering episodes behind him, Ishan had learnt his lesson. But I was wrong. Some people thrive on complications, and when there are none, they seem to go out of their way to create problems for themselves. Even though Ishan had served his six-month ban from playing international cricket for using steroids, I had my doubts if the ghosts from his past could be vanquished so easily. His travails, after all, went back a long way.

About three years ago, the Indian team's performance, with Amod as captain, started plummeting. So lacklustre was the performance of key Indian players, that suddenly tongues started wagging about the re-appearance of betting and match-fixing. It was against this background that Ishan pulled out of the team on the eve of two very crucial matches. On one occasion, he backed out of an ODI against Australia citing a stomach ache. On the second occasion, he complained of severe headache and dizziness just before the game started. Both times, medical examinations showed nothing, making people suspect that something was amiss.

Ishan's behaviour, thus, had become a contentious issue. Six months later, while selecting the team for an upcoming game against the touring Englishmen, at least two of the five selectors strongly rooted for his exclusion. I was captain then, and I supported his inclusion because I thought it was important to keep a match winner like him in the team. Ishan made it into the team, and because I'd had a hand in his inclusion, I knew I had invited pressure onto myself.

Later that year, we toured South Africa. In our first Test at Johannesburg, we had gained a slender first innings lead of 56 runs. This was really encouraging, considering the Johannesburg wicket is known to aid pace bowling. Now the onus was on our pacers to ensure that South Africa was restricted to a low score in the second innings. However, Ishan bowled one of his most reckless spells, giving away 42 runs in just 5 overs, with 6 no-balls and 2 wides. At the end of that spell, he complained of dizziness and went off the field. Subsequently, he did not bowl again, and we ended up losing the match.

Routine medical tests were carried out on Ishan again, and again all seemed well, except that his blood pressure was slightly on the lower side. I had a chat with Ishan and he said he was tense as he had just heard that his grandmother was unwell. Giving him the benefit of the doubt, I left the matter at that. I hoped the fighter in Ishan would goad him to compensate for the way he had bowled.

He did practise hard in the nets for the next three days. But again, when it came to the day of the actual match, he let us down again. I won the toss at Cape Town and chose to field. Just minutes before we were to take the field, Ishan began to look like a bundle of nerves. His body was trembling when I went up to him; he was standing alone in a corner of the dressing room.

'What happened? Are you okay?' I asked.

Ishan fumbled for an answer.

'Will you tell me what the problem is?' I demanded.

At least five other cricketers and Dave had come up and stood behind me, all equally bewildered. I took Ishan's wrist in my hand; his heart rate seemed to be racing.

'Listen,' Dave said, 'half the cricketers are already out on the field. Can we just leave Ishan aside and pick another pacer?'

I looked at the clock on the wall. There was just one minute left before the scheduled start of play. And, indeed, there was no other option but to go through the formalities of making this last-minute change. Usually, changes in the team are not allowed after the toss, but the South African captain was kind enough to agree. The game started five minutes behind schedule. It did cause us some embarrassment, as also considerable worry, because Ishan's replacement, Nayan, was a rookie.

We didn't fare too badly that day, bowling out the South Africans for 243. But I couldn't get Ishan out of my mind. I knew that the team couldn't afford to tolerate his unstable behaviour any longer – some action needed to be taken. And, in standing by him, my own credentials had come under the scanner. By lunchtime, I was told that an Indian news channel had been beaming a story hinting that both Ishan and I could be hand-in-glove and part of a betting syndicate. I had to fix this issue once and for all.

After the day's play, I sent one of the junior players to Ishan's room and asked him to get Ishan to the snooker room. Playing snooker was a de-stressing technique some of us adopted.

When Ishan arrived, he looked even more nervous than he had in the morning. This was possibly because I looked much angrier than I had in the morning.

I took the first shot. The blue ball went straight into the netted hole. It was Ishan's turn. He missed. I hit two more shots, both into the net. Ishan missed twice again.

'Why are you sweating? The room is air conditioned,' I said.

Ishan didn't answer. He pulled out a handkerchief to wipe his face; as he did so, a small packet with white powder fell. I bent down and picked it up.

'What's this?'

Ishan started shaking.

'I asked you something!' I shouted. 'What is this?'

Asad, who was perhaps passing the snooker room and heard my raised voice, peeped in to see if everything was all right.

'Asad, go. Leave us alone,' I said curtly. Asad immediately closed the door behind him.

I locked the door and walked up to Ishan, 'Look, nothing about you surprises me anymore. But I need to know the truth. If you don't tell me what's going on, I'm going to the board and telling them I suspect you're taking drugs.'

Ishan broke down, 'Coke. That's cocaine.'

I'd thought as much, although I'd had only the slightest brush with it almost twelve years ago.

I had just returned from Kenya where I'd gone with the India A side. It had been a six-week tour, and as soon as our flight landed in Delhi, I went to Indraprastha College, where my then girlfriend, Ritwika, was a final year student. Surprisingly, Ritwika was not in town. One of her friends told me she had gone to Rishikesh for the day. I was surprised when I heard this. Yes, Ritwika tended to be absentminded, and very impulsive, but how had she forgotten the date I was coming back on?

Ritwika returned late that evening. I was furious, but Ritwika was unruffled, 'Come on, Mayank. Did you tell me what time your flight was arriving? Besides, it's just a matter of a few hours. I'm back now. So, chill.'

Not for the first time I wondered why I was in the relationship. We were such different people. I did love her; and she told me a hundred times that she loved me, but I was never really sure she did, because she so often did things she must have known would hurt me.

'So, who did you go to Rishikesh with?' I asked, not wanting to fight. Of late, it seemed it was all we did.

'This guy, Sanjay, I met recently. You should meet him, he's great fun.'

I kept quiet, trying not to feel jealous as she continued to chat about the trip and Sanjay.

Over the next two days, Ritwika seemed distracted; and she seemed to be receiving an unusual number of calls. The night before I was to leave for Jamshedpur, I was taking a shower when I suddenly heard Ritwika scream. I rushed out.

'Stop it! Stop stalking me!' she shouted and banged the phone down. She was shaking, I reached her.

'What is it, Ritwika? Who was that?'

'Sanjay.'

'Sanjay? The guy you went to Rishikesh with?'

Ritwika looked down in embarrassment.

'But what does he want?'

'He's harassing me for some money I owe him. He paid for some cocaine we did in Rishikesh. I told him I'd give it to him next month –'

'What?' I couldn't believe what I was hearing. 'What do you mean? You tried cocaine?'

'Well, he had some with him, and I thought I'd give it a try.'

'But ... but why?'

'Why? What do you mean why?' She seemed genuinely puzzled. Seeing my expression she continued, 'It's not a big deal, Mayank. I just wanted to try it once.'

'Ritwika, I don't understand. Why would you want to try something that messes up your system? That could get you addicted? And why would you try it with someone you barely know?'

She shrugged, 'I don't know, I wasn't thinking about it that much.'

'Did you think how I might react?'

She looked at me. I think we both knew at the same moment that we had taken the relationship as far as it could go.

I left for Jamshedpur the next day. We kept in touch for a while, but the calls slowly petered out, and by the end of that year, completely stopped.

I guess Ritwika was just someone who didn't think too much about the consequences. Her tryst with drugs was possibly something that happened because of mere curiosity, and hopefully, it ended before it really began. Ishan's drug abuse, though, was an attempt to fill a gap caused by circumstances that would have adversely affected even a much stronger person.

'I was born into a lower middle class family,' Ishan began. 'We lived in Mahim. My grandfather was a peon in a government office, and he wanted my father to work as a clerk in the same place. My father, however, wanted to be a cricketer, and he decided to drop out of school, so that he could concentrate on the game. He was a strong middle-order batsman and he made quite a mark for himself in domestic cricket in the early eighties. But he never made it into the Indian side.

'After six seasons in domestic cricket, it seemed unlikely that my father would ever break into the side. You know how hard it was financially in those days, if a cricketer didn't make it to the national side. Meanwhile, a good friend of his, an all-rounder, made it into the side. This probably increased my father's frustration. He took to drinking. And then, he met with a road accident that crippled his right leg permanently. I am told my mother was pregnant when this accident happened. Two months later, I was born.

'My father eventually started working as a mechanic in a nearby garage, but whatever little money he earned, he splurged on alcohol. And then, he found out that his friend and ... and my mother were having an affair.'

Ishan looked anguished. He paused for a second and then went on, 'My parents had an acrimonious, rather violent separation. One night, it was raining really hard; I'm told that my father beat my mother till she was forced to run away. I was at my aunt's place two lanes away when this happened. My mother left and never returned. We heard that some people had died in the storm, so when we couldn't find her for a week, the family assumed she too had died that night.

'My aunt raised me after that. Initially, I would pass the garage my father worked in on my way to school. He tried to speak to me a couple of times, but I blamed him for my mother's death, so I would just ignore him. Soon I started taking a different route to school. Now and then, my father, in his desperation to reach me, would make a scene outside my aunt's house. Finally, my uncle spoke to him, and from that day onwards, my father left me alone. I must have been fourteen then.

'On my new route home from school, I would see a strange assortment of people from between Mahim station and Matunga Road station. I noticed one of them in particular – he looked like a snoopy sidekick to a villain in a B-grade Hindi movie of the '80s, whose eyes were always bloodshot and beard untrimmed. He would always be sniffing some stuff laid out on a silver paper. One day, he noticed me staring, and responded with a smile and a gesture inviting me to join him. I was scared and ran away. I told my aunt about these people and was admonished and advised to stay away from them.

'Meanwhile, my cricket was going quite well. My school sports teacher had persuaded my aunt to let me join cricket practice at Shivaji Park and I would go there after school. One day, out of the blue, I learned something that shattered me completely. The school authorities told me my fees for the month had not been paid. The accountant asked me to find out about it from the same cricketer who happened to be my father's friend. I was puzzled. I went home and asked my aunt and uncle why the cricketer had been paying my school fees. It was then that my uncle told me that I was not my father's son. My biological father was that cricketer.'

For a few moments, there was a deafening silence. Ishan gave a rueful laugh and shook his head, 'I was fifteen then. Can you imagine what that information did to me?

'The next day, after practice, I got down from the bus and started walking home in the dark. For some reason, I was reluctant to go home. Suddenly, someone tapped me on my shoulder. I turned; it was the villainous sidekick, smiling at me. Up close, he looked terrible. His eyes were red and swollen. His fingers were trembling. On any other day, I would have probably run away; but that day I was too numb to react to anything.

'His name was D'Souza, he said, and he just wanted to be friends with me. We spent the next few minutes chatting below a streetlight. Soon enough, I realised why he was making an effort with me. He asked me if I had five rupees because he wanted to treat me to something I'd never had before. I gave him a five-rupee note and he led me into one of those extremely narrow alleys that separate two rows of shanties. He stopped at one of the tiny shanties and called out for someone. There was some whispering, and an exchange of money for something that D'Souza then handed to me.

'I opened the wrapped paper and what I saw was some powder. I asked him what it was and he said it was called crystal meth or ice. "Sniff it", he told me, and I did. Within minutes, I was experiencing the most extraordinary, terrifying hallucinations. As a local train passed by behind us in the distance, I imagined the train was crushing me. I have a phobia of cockroaches, and as I spotted one nearby, I saw, suddenly, hundreds of them coming towards me. I spent the night in that dirty alley, going mad with fear. The next morning, I promised myself that I would never try something like that again. I went back home, and told my aunt and uncle that I'd felt too ill to come all the way home and had stayed with a friend.'

'What happened then?' I asked.

'I didn't try anything again for almost four years. By then I'd broken into the Under-19 Mumbai side, and then into the Ranji side. At that time, I was also playing for a Dadar club. My performance was quite good, and I knew that a senior pacer, Gawli, was not happy about this, perhaps because he himself hadn't been playing too well for a while. One day after a crucial club match that we won, Gawli suddenly became quite friendly towards me. He said he and another player, Ramakant, were going out to celebrate, and I should join them. Surprisingly, the curator of our pitch, Mhatre, also joined us. With Mhatre directing him, Gawli drove into the Dharavi area.

'I wondered what sort of celebration we could have at Dharavi. My hunch was that these guys were looking for prostitutes. I didn't dare ask them, though; I suppose I felt I was too much of a junior to actually confront them. It was already quite dark by then. Mhatre soon led us to a spot that frightened me. I could see some men hanging out in clusters. One group of about three men were sniffing, what I was told later, a mixture of burnt reptile and tobacco. Gawli took this powder from the men, sniffed it, and then handed it to me. I'll never know why, but I too sniffed it.

'Later, on our way back, Gawli asked me if I had enjoyed it. To be honest, the high had been quite good, but I felt awful that I'd broken the promise I had made to myself. Gawli tried to cheer me up, "Hey, listen, we needed something to break the ice between us. And we are in a high-pressure profession; indulging in these occasional pleasures is harmless. Trust me, we never do the hard drugs that will stop us from taking the cricket field the next day."

'My uncle had often told me that there was one thing common between my father and me – we were both extremely weak people. Perhaps, he was right. I got carried away by what Gawli said. The addictive substances we experimented with were very strange. For example, we mixed the pain killing ointment Iodex with jam and ate that with bread. Or we would try these tablets that are usually given to women about to deliver. Paying the chemist an extra hundred bucks would make them easily available to us.

'This went on for about a year. And I got sick of doing these things. More importantly, I was being considered for selection in the Indian side and I knew that if I had to actually make it, I would have to rethink my priorities. I decided to give it all up.

'Soon I earned my first India cap. The sense of pride was overwhelming. I could feel the change it brought about in me as a person. I believed that I had finally left my past behind.'

'So, what happened?'

'We were in Delhi for an Irani Trophy match. The only other national-level player was Jeet. On the evening before the match, Jeet took me to the hotel's disco. Some half a dozen girls soon surrounded us and we all danced together. Then Jeet went to a corner with one of these girls; he seemed to know her. I saw him talking to a man, and then he and the girl left.

'By the time I managed to get rid of the girls who had surrounded me, and followed Jeet to his room, half an hour had passed. I walked in, only to see Jeet and the girl about to sniff some white powder he'd laid out on the table. When he saw me, he asked me to join them. I asked him what the powder was. He told me it was cocaine, and that it would make me feel wonderful.

'So I had cocaine for the first time that night, and the effect really was mind-blowing. It filled me up with incredible energy. At around 11.30 p.m., I told Jeet I was going to my room because we had to get up early for the next day's match. Jeet laughed. "The effect has only begun. It won't let you sleep," he told me. Then he increased the volume of the music that was playing and all three of us began to dance. Before I knew it, Jeet and the girl started making out; I went out and got that girl, Renny, whom I had danced with, into the room. We danced till nearly four in the morning, and then, I returned to my room with Renny. I wasn't feeling even a bit tired. I desperately wanted to make love to her, but she stopped me. "Fifteen thousand," she said. I was stunned. "If you want the clothes removed, that comes for a price," she added.

'She didn't budge from the figure and agreed only after I promised to pay her. And later, when I walked onto the cricket field, I still felt as energised as ever, the added.'

'So, this girl you took to bed – was a call girl?' I asked.

'No, no. She was a college student, studying in second year.'

Ishan went on, 'That evening Jeet told me he'd been taking coke for a couple of years. Apparently, a huge number of celebrities took coke because of stress and also because they could then put in extra hours at work.'

'What?' I asked, surprised.

'Yes. The next time you see an ageing actor suddenly flash his toned, muscular body, remember, it doesn't happen so easily and naturally. So, Jeet said he did it only once in a while, say once in a month or so. And the next time Jeet and I were on tour – it was two days before a Test in Mumbai, I remember – I paid for the coke.'

'How many players in our team have been doing cocaine?' I asked out of concern.

'Well, if you count the regulars, I would say it's only Jeet and I, but at least three other cricketers do it off and on. Including Amod.'

I shook my head, 'Don't you know how dangerous these drugs are? Don't you want to stop?'

'Yes, bhai, that's the problem: I am trying to quit. That's why I've been playing so badly; it's the withdrawal symptoms. About eight months ago, Jeet, Baljeet and I went to this rave party. It was at this Mehrauli farmhouse that Baljeet's singer friend, Sukhbir, owns. We were surprised to find at least half a dozen B-list actresses and models there. There were also a few cricketers who played for the Delhi and Punjab Ranji trophy teams. We partied all night after getting high on Ecstasy and LSD. But one of the Delhi players, Harsh, started puking and then, fell unconscious. We had a horrible time getting him treated and covering up the whole thing. It really upset me, and I haven't had drugs since.'

I nodded. We talked about what kind of support he might need, medically and emotionally, to stay off drugs. Suddenly, I remembered something. 'Who is this ex-cricketer who is your father?' I asked.

For a moment, Ishan fumbled. It was obviously something he had hoped I might not ask.

'You don't have to tell me if you'd rather not,' I added quickly.

Ishan shook his head; he drank a glass of water and then said, 'Sharath Jaidev.'

I was flabbergasted. Sharath Jaidev, one of the more elegant left-handed batsmen of his times, was now a commentator with a sports channel. And as a commentator, he consistently criticised the Indian team. There was no decision of mine that had not invited an adverse comment from him. I have always valued constructive criticism, but in him, I've seen a peculiar frustration – something that makes him pick on far too many people far too often.

For all his talent, Jaidev was accused of selfishness; it was said that he only played for records. For that matter, I would still consider him an extremely selfish man: he had been offered the job of coach and with all his sharp insights, I do feel he could make a worthy coach. But, instead, he chose to remain in the safe comfort of the commentary box.

Just then something occurred to me. 'Haven't you bumped into each other even once over these last six years?' I asked Ishan.

'Yes. From the moment I made it to the national side, I wanted to meet him at least once. It was only after a year though, that I finally managed to pin him down in Sri Lanka.'

'And what he did he say?'

'Nothing.'

'Nothing?'

'I don't know what I was looking for, from him. And I suppose he didn't know what to say when I asked him why ... why he hadn't bothered about my mother or me. He just patted me on my shoulder and walked away. That day I knew, once and forever, that I would be happier if I erased any thought of him from my mind.'

I went up to Ishan and hugged him. There was so much he had been through.

24 June 2008

It's 4.40 p.m. I see Raghav and Vinod walking towards me.

'This is just ridiculous,' Vinod says in anger as he reaches me. 'Raghav just told me about the match-fixing rumours. I think the Australians are behind it.'

'I don't know, Vinod; Raghav heard about the match-fixing from reliable sources.'

But Vinod is convinced. He says that perhaps one of their ex-cricketers, who is currently the coach of a domestic side in India, got in touch with the concerned bookie and asked him to, then, get in touch with Tiwari and leak this story.

I think about Vinod's theory. I trust his knowledge and judgement. If what he says is true, huge amounts of money must have exchanged hands.

'Dude,' Vinod continues, 'if you want to win tomorrow, just forget about the issue. Trust me, the team you have is a good one; the players have great commitment and would never think of throwing a final away. It's all crap, a ploy to distract you guys because the Aussies are scared of you.'

I'd like to think Vinod is right. After all, in the last twenty-four hours or so, cricket has been relegated to an insignificant zone in my mind.

I get back to practice. For the next two-and-a-half hours, I bat and field; and if I'm not doing either, I keep an eye on the other players. I want Asad to play a lot straighter; I want Amod to cut and pull as hard as he can; and I want Rajat to bowl a fuller length. For the most part, I'm able to exorcise the ghosts from my mind; yet, the moment I spot a less than all-out effort by any of the players, a flicker of doubt springs in my mind.

In the evening, I sit in the hotel's coffee shop. It's still some forty-five minutes to go before we assemble for dinner. Despite the optimism I've been trying to generate in the last few hours, parts of my report come back to me; those parts that have the closest and most direct connection with the issue that is the cause of my anguish.

✦

14

June 2007

While Baljeet has managed to rein in his activities to some extent, Jeet is just incorrigible. Jeet hails from a rich business family in Baroda; his father owns a pharmaceutical company. Having been brought up in a palatial house, he is extremely pampered; apparently a chauffeur-driven Toyota used to take him to cricket practice. The riches and privileges that Jeet has enjoyed from birth, however, have not affected his competitive spirit. In fact, he must have inherited a hunger to win from his father, a self-made man who started off as a small time medical representative.

When Jeet first arrived on the one-day scene five years ago, he was hailed as one of the brightest new talents on the horizon. Some pundits had even compared his stroke-play with that of Richards and Sobers; nobody could deny that he was one of the most naturally gifted players. On a good day, he could turn a game around in just a few overs. Moreover, Jeet's body language exuded great confidence. Not once would he appear daunted, even when he faced the quickest of pace bowlers at the raw age of nineteen. He was also a terrific fielder. Where he lacked, though, was application. After a half century, his concentration would wither. There would be flashy, lofted shots that often made it appear as though he was giving fielders some catching practice. Initially, these problems were attributed to the naiveté of youth. Since the board saw a lot of potential in him otherwise, they were patient in his case and kept motivating him by giving him additional responsibilities. However, three years later, the board and the senior players began to feel that Jeet's batting hadn't really progressed.

Apart from this, what invited criticism was his behaviour off the field. In some way, I do hold him guilty for popularising nightclub culture in the team. He was quite addicted to visiting these clubs, and would always look out for colleagues to join him whenever possible. The players who joined him in his adventures from time to time included Rajat, Baljeet and Ishan. In fact, Rajat, a long established pacer in the side, had once come to me, petrified that he'd been infected with HIV. Apparently, he and Jeet had been out partying, each returning to the hotel room with a prostitute. Rajat's condom had got torn during the night, and he was now scared that he might have become HIV positive. Along with the team manager, I had a Rapid HIV Test run on Rajat, and fortunately, he was found to be clear. Thankfully, this scare served as a wake-up call for Rajat.

While these three cricketers' performances were sometimes affected by their late night escapades, Jeet's energy levels never dipped after a night of partying. I remember how he partied late into the night and yet always managed to come out the next morning firing on all cylinders. In Australia, three years ago, he hit a century and took us to victory single-handedly in a one-day match. The night before, he had been out in a pub till well after midnight. How and why the team management had allowed his late night adventures, perhaps, had something to do with the fact that he happened to be Amod's blue-eyed boy when Amod was captain. I suspected that there was probably another reason why Amod was so soft on Jeet: from time to time, Jeet arranged girls for Amod in his hotel room.

Once I became captain, I didn't really feel the need to meddle in Jeet's lifestyle as it didn't seem to affect his performance. The only change I brought about was a rule that all members of the team had to be in their hotel rooms by 10.30 p.m. on the eve of a match the next day and during a Test match. And Jeet didn't seem to mind.

The crisis occurred last summer, when an airhostess with British Airways came out in the media with accusations that Jeet had been harassing her with lewd text messages for three months. The airhostess, Julia, said she had met Jeet on a flight to London where he was heading to consult a doctor about a knee injury. She said they'd gone out for a drink, after which she'd returned home and the lewd messages had started.

Some of these texts were reproduced in a newspaper; the journalist had also done some research and realised that a few of the messages had been sent during a Test match, while Jeet was padded up and waiting in the pavilion for his turn to bat. As captain of the side, I found it deeply embarrassing that one of my players should be embroiled in such a scandal.

When Jeet faced me after this, he looked apologetic. He walked up to me remorsefully, 'Mayank, I'm sorry. I just got carried away.' Well, neither of us really wanted to talk about it, though I was slightly relieved that Jeet had acknowledged his folly.

Over the next few months, Jeet seemed to be more sober when we were playing. He would spend his time training in the hotel pool or the gym, instead of in night clubs as had been his wont. He also seemed to have found a steady girlfriend finally, model and Miss India runner-up, Sheetal Baweja. Both would chat for hours once our day's practice was over. In a way, I was glad. I thought Sheetal would bring about a steadying influence on Jeet.

But I was wrong. During the World Cup last year, there was a phase when the team was rather precariously poised. Having performed poorly in our initial matches, it was imperative that we win the match against West Indies to stay in the tournament. The four days in the run-up to the match was a time I can never forget. We were all extremely nervous and under great pressure. Dave, our coach, undertook long sessions with each player, trying to instil confidence in us. Let me add here that at this time, Dave and I weren't on the best of terms. Of late, I had been finding him high-handed and autocratic. Moreover, he seemed vindictive towards the senior players. Even the media reported how he would persistently vouch for some uncapped players and badmouth the seniors. All this had, no doubt, created some amount of friction between us. Yet, I swallowed my ego and rallied behind him in preparing us for this do-or-die encounter.

The night before the day-night match, I was feeling quite edgy. I had six possible case scenarios floating in my mind – three if we batted first and three if we batted second. One move I was pretty clear about, was to shuffle the batting order a bit and surprise the opposition. Shreyas was yet to recover completely from his viral infection. And with rookie Rajiv Raina having played that brilliant knock against Zimbabwe, I thought it would be better to rest Shreyas for this encounter. I wasn't sure though if Rajiv could be sent first down against the Windies. I'd much rather have him preserved for the late overs' slog. My gut feeling was that if Jeet came in at number three and came good, we'd be able to score a lot faster and take the steam out of the bowling attack.

It was 11.30 p.m. I wondered if it was a good time to speak to Jeet about this. I decided to try my luck as Jeet was known to stay up late.

I rang the bell of Jeet's hotel room and could hear some murmurs inside, which made me doubly sure he was awake. I assumed he was on the phone. When he didn't open the door, I rang the bell again and then twice more.

Jeet finally opened the door. He was panting for breath and I wondered why.

'What happened? Is everything okay?' I enquired.

'Yes . . . yes. All's well,' Jeet fumbled with his clothes as he replied. He acted as though he'd been awoken from a deep sleep.

'You were talking to someone?'

'Oh, yeah. I was talking to Sheetal . . . on the phone. You wanted to discuss something?'

'I just thought of a change in our match strategy that I wanted to discuss with you.'

'Yeah, sure.'

'You'll bat at number three and get on with your natural game, irrespective of what the situation is.'

Jeet nodded, but seemed preoccupied. This was important though, so I continued, 'Somehow, Shreyas has been unable to find gaps early on and it allows the bowlers to get on top. Your job will be to unsettle the bowling plan of the Windies.'

Just as I finished my sentence, to my utter shock, two girls barged out of Jeet's washroom, both in a state of partial undress. One was shouting at the other, 'Fucking bitch! You think I want to make out with you?'

'Don't pretend like you're so innocent,' the other screamed back.

The first girl then turned to Jeet and said, 'Where do you get such creepy sluts from? No sooner did we get in than she started acting fresh with me.'

Jeet was blushing a shade of deep beetroot as he glanced at me. He persuaded the girls to leave, and both were so upset, they did. Jeet turned and looked at me.

'Good progress, dude. So when did you graduate to threesomes?' I asked him.

'Mayank . . . ,' he began.

'Save it. The only reason I'm concerned is that we have a match tomorrow. I cannot believe we have someone like you on the side. Do you have no idea how important tomorrow's match is for us?' I was shouting now.

'It . . . it just helps me beat stress. That's why I did it,' he said pleadingly.

I shook my head. I couldn't believe he took his place in the national team so much for granted. 'You're out of the team for tomorrow's game,' I said, and walked away.

Early next morning, our keeper Aslam came to my room, to discuss some ideas he had for the game. Aslam was one of the few members of the side I could trust implicitly – such was his regard for work ethics. Aslam's deft keeping was, perhaps, one of the redeeming features of our performance in the World Cup.

I told him what had happened the previous night.

Aslam thought for a few minutes and then said in his usual measured way, 'The problem is, we can't afford to go into such a crucial match without him.'

I nodded; I was calmer with the passage of the night, and I knew the truth of what he was saying. I decided to go to Jeet's room and tell him he would be playing.

Jeet's door was open; he was in the shower. He called out to say he'd be out in five minutes so I sat down to wait. A diary caught my attention.

I don't really know what made me pick it up and flip through it. Normally, I would never have invaded anyone's privacy like that, but perhaps I was seeking to understand how Jeet operated. I flipped through the pages: there were cricketing tips that the Australian great, Marsh, had given Jeet; some details of one of Jeet's sponsorship deals. And then, I came across a paragraph that made me stop in my tracks:

Zimbabwe, 2004. Saw a blue film on a local cable channel, that had a guy make love to two women. Two days later, I tried this out myself. Man, it was awesome. Got to try this again!

My next opportunity came at this bar in Barbados. I met this gorgeous young woman. She seemed to like me a lot. The conversation quickly turned to how much we'd like to get a room together. As we left the bar to go to my hotel, she asked – 'as an afterthought' – if it would be all right to bring her young friend. Her smile left little to the imagination.

Man! My fantasy was going to be fulfilled again, and without my making any extra effort for it! This time, I sniffed a bit of cocaine, which made the experience all the more mind-blowing. It was the best sex I ever had. I knew I was going to repeat the experience again. It was that awesome, man!

I closed the book slowly. What kind of discussion could I have with Jeet? Just then, he walked out of the bathroom.

He opened his mouth to speak, but I stopped him with a gesture. 'The team needs you. Unfortunately. You're playing today.'

I walked out, hoping that whatever little sense of responsibility Jeet had left in him would make him rise to the occasion.

Jeet did get a decent 43 off 49, after being let off twice, in an otherwise rather embarrassing show by our batsmen.

I couldn't help feeling what I've always felt about him. He was a lucky bastard to get away with things the way he always managed to do.

24 June 2008

It's six in the morning. I have spent the whole night reading the report I'd prepared the previous year. I am bleary eyed and drowsy, yet there's too much on my mind, preventing me from sleeping. As I think of Baljeet and Jeet, I find that the one thing that is common between them is that they live for the day. They are impulsive, at times extremely so. But as far as their integrity goes, on the field, they're hard fighters. True, their performance has been affected by indulgences they've found difficult to resist. Yes, they tend to be an easy prey to temptation – whether in the form of wine, women or drugs. But would they indulge in something on purpose? I doubt it. I don't believe a bookmaker could sway them.

I'm confused. I wonder if this exercise is resulting in anything except more chaos. Revathi is perhaps right. I think a lot because of which I can't be at peace – ever.

I look at my watch. I'm tempted to call Revathi. It's about ten in the morning in India. I call her; she is on her way to court.

'I was just thinking of calling you, but thought you'd be asleep,' she says brightly, the sound of her voice instantly lifting my spirits. 'Slept well?'

Revathi knows I can get a bit too pumped up before important matches and end up staying awake. For some reason, I don't want her to know what has happened – that there are rumours that a couple of my colleagues have been paid off by bookies.

'Yes, just woke a bit early and thought I'd speak to you.'

We talk about our son Ayush, my parents and then about cricket, strictly in that order. I tell her about my idea of including Naved Khan on the team. I usually tend to take Revathi into confidence on any cricketing dilemmas plaguing me, whether she is equipped to help or not. She thinks it is a good idea and I trust her instincts. I consider talking about the possible match fixing. However, that doesn't happen. Revathi is preoccupied with an important case she's working on, and I think it is unfair to broach the topic in her current state of distraction.

We wish each other luck and end the conversation. I feel lonely, with just my thoughts for company.

✦

15

QUEENS PARK OVAL, PORT OF SPAIN

20 June 2007

Windies Bowlers Ring India's Death Knell

West Indian bowlers fought back from a blistering opening by Asad Iqbal to snatch an exciting eleven-run victory, marking the end of India's World Cup hopes.

The 31 wides that were awarded to the West Indians, allowing them to reach 281, proved costly for the Indians, but the real turning point came when Joel Harper bowled Mayank Pradhan for 82 in the 47th over of the chase. Desmond Welch followed up the next ball by throwing down the stumps at the striker's end to run out Aslam Khan.

Initially, India appeared to be cruising with ten overs remaining. A brisk 43 by Jeet Gohil off just 35 balls had put them virtually on top. The asking rate had dropped to around 6.5, they had six wickets in hand, and with a calm Mayank at the crease, victory seemed certain. However, things turned around in the 41st over. A mistimed attempt to clear the long-on boundary had Jeet caught in the deep off Harper. And then, as keeper Aslam Khan struggled to rotate the strike, the required run-rate gradually increased.

Harper removed Aslam when Patrick Haynes stumped him off a wide for 17 from 29 balls, but the wicket of Mayank was the killer blow. He seemed to have paced his innings to perfection, pushing singles and twos and finding the occasional boundary and setting himself for a late assault. However, he backed away trying to hit Welch through the off side when boundaries were needed and was bowled.

The Windies pace duo of Carl Patterson and Desmond Welch bowled superbly in the dying stages. Too much was left to do for Rajat Shetty and Baljeet Khurana, who had to find 22 runs from the last two overs and then 15 from Harper's final six balls. Despite an early scare, when Rajat drove the first ball for four, Harper fired in a succession of low full tosses that gave the Indians little chance to reach their target. India's defeat has left behind a pall of gloom as sponsors brace themselves to cope with some heavy losses.

West Indies 281 for 4 (Andy Morton 79, Simon Richards 50*) off fifty overs beat **India** 270 for 7 off fifty overs (Mayank Pradhan 82, Asad Iqbal 56, Jeet 43) by eleven runs.

◆

The Windies' win, thus, put paid to our World Cup dream. What was particularly shameful was that our side was out of the Cup, right at the preliminary stage. And this happened despite our collective experience and talent being unmatched by any other side. Today, when I look back, I can say without an iota of doubt that this defeat marked the saddest day of my life. It threw up questions I may never be able to answer satisfactorily all my life. It resulted in some ghosts haunting me forever.

I knew my report would be incomplete without bringing up the inescapable devil of betting and match-fixing. Ironically, this also happens to be the issue I'm most clueless about. The thing is, unless there is absolute proof, figuring out whether a player has been bought is as difficult as determining whether two people have had an affair. For all you know, they might only have flirted with each other, or indulged in foreplay. There are players who are guilty of having leaked invaluable, confidential information, gathered during team meetings, to friends who were actually bookmakers. These players can't really be booked for match fixing because, one, in legal terms, mere sharing of information, in many cases, is not tantamount to fixing the outcome of the match. Two, almost all bookmakers have cover-up professions. As such, players, at times genuinely so, are unaware of a particular individual's betting links. Hence the analogy; several cricketers may have indulged in the foreplay of match-fixing, but may not necessarily have consummated the act. However, the seriousness of the offence, insofar as my personal opinion is concerned, remains the same.

In all my playing years, I can only recollect one known instance of a player from our side aiding bookies.

Around 1999-2000, on a tour of Australia, Shreyas happened to be my roommate. Sometimes, I overheard him give details about the pitch over the phone. When I asked Shreyas what was going on, he said, 'I'm only passing on trivial information about the way the pitch will behave or about the weather conditions. What's wrong in that? I have never under-performed in a match.'

At that point, I couldn't think of anything wrong with it either. Besides, an ICB official who had accompanied the team as its media manager, was aware of Shreyas' calls too, but didn't say anything to him about it. So I kept quiet. It only made sense a year later, when Shreyas performed dismally at a very crucial stage of a match against West Indies, which we eventually lost. When I discussed his performance with an ex-cricketer mentioning what Shreyas had done in Australia, the teammate said, 'Why would anybody offer a cricketer money for exchange of trivial information like the weather and the wicket, which can be obtained from anyone? It's just a trap bookies use. They tempt a cricketer with a huge amount of money for information, which appears harmless. Later, they tempt him with more money and ask for information that's confidential. The money offered multiplies progressively and the player gets trapped. He knows his career or even his life could be in grave danger if he backs out now.'

Till date, when I think of the Shreyas episode in the context of what this ex-cricketer said, I feel guilty for not reporting him earlier. For all the matches that we lost in those days and where Shreyas was not at his best, the fear of his complicity in those defeats would haunt me forever.

Over the years, I have heard of some rather innovative ways in which cricketers have helped bookies. One cricketer would rub and adjust his left pad repeatedly before getting out. Another famous cricketer's cousin is said to have indulged in betting. This cousin would park himself in the stands and start accepting bets, after the cricketer reached ninety, on whether or not the cricketer would hit a century. The cricketer would significantly slow down his game between ninety and hundred to facilitate maximum pooling in of money.

Then, there were instances when cricketers received lavish gifts from rather dubious sources. A cameraperson, who happened to be a friend and who, at one point, was working with a leading sports channel, informed me how former captain Sharad's fetish for fancy watches saw him being gifted some very expensive watches by people rumoured to have links with match-fixing. These watches were often carried into the country by this cameraperson in the bags in which he kept his camera equipment. When I look back, I do recall that Sharad, at one stage of his career, showed a bizarre tendency to start off his innings well, but invariably getting himself run out at crucial junctures. On a few occasions, he got his partner run out. Whether these run-outs and the watches had a direct co-relation remains a matter of conjecture.

By the time I made it to the national team in the nineties, cricket had begun to be talked about for the wrong reasons. Whenever a team lost an important match, cricketers would be suspected of foul play. While there was no denying the existence of the practice, it was perhaps prevalent on a lesser scale than was being speculated.

The problem first came to the fore in India when a leading journalist alleged that a bookmaker had offered him a huge amount of money to introduce him to an Indian cricketer. Taking a cue from that, a magazine did an interview with a former cricketer, who made some damning allegations against one of his teammates. Various inquiry commissions across countries – the King Commission in South Africa, the Justice Qayyum Commission in Pakistan – found that match-fixing had actually taken place. The Chandrachud Commission in India was relatively evasive on the issue and was even accused of covering up facts.

Former South African captain Hansie Cronje's confessions of not being 'entirely honest' were made on 15 June 2000, in a statement that also revealed the full extent of his contact with bookmakers. This list included Mukesh Gupta, who was introduced to him by Mohammad Azharuddin in 1996, during the third Test in Kanpur. Gupta gave Cronje thirty thousand dollars to persuade the South Africans to lose wickets on the last day to lose the match. The former captain said he did not convey the offer to the South Africans, but as South Africa lost anyway, he decided to keep the money. At this point, Cronje was hooked. The offers started to come in and the amounts increased. During the reciprocal tour, Cronje received fifty thousand dollars from Gupta for passing on team information.

In the 2000 Centurion Test, Cronje was contacted by a Marlon Arenstam, who identified himself as a cricket lover who worked for NSI, a sports betting company. He said he would give Cronje five hundred thousand rand for the charity of his choice together with a gift if Cronje declared and made a game of it. After the match, Arenstam visited Cronje, giving him fifty thousand rand in two tranches, along with a leather jacket. The promised half a million rand did not materialise though. Cronje also admitted asking Pieter Strydom to place a fifty rand bet on South Africa to win for him.

Before a one-day series in India, Cronje received numerous calls from a 'Sanjay' asking to fix a match. Cronje had long since reached the point of no return. Sanjay did not let up and Cronje tried to get rid of him, he claims, by giving him the names of Gibbs, Strydom and Nicky Boje before the third ODI. This, Cronje believed, is one of the conversations taped by the New Delhi police.

And then there was Imran Khan's statement before the Qayyum Commission:

Imran Ahmed Khan Niazi S/O Ikram Ullah Khan
(Recorded on 11 November 1998)

I was captain from 1982 to 1992 except for a few occasions when I was unfit. During the period I played cricket, one incident I should mention is that in India, while Asif Iqbal was captain, there was some allegation that there was betting on a Test. Asif Iqbal had declared the innings at a stage when Pakistan had not scored more runs than India. There were rumours that it was a bet on who would score more runs in the first innings. In 1989, during the Australasia cup, Javed Miandad rang me up that four of our players have been sold out. It was the final, and whatever money we had won in the side matches, we made a bet of that on Pakistan winning and we won the match. On another occasion, one of the players levelled allegations against Miandad while he was playing in the World Cup but that was not believable as no single player can fix a match. As match-fixing involves guaranteeing the result, whosoever are the good players of the team must be implicated. And, without the knowledge or consent of the captain, no team can indulge in match-fixing. I believe match-fixing has taken place as players have made allegations, including the current captain (Sohail). Moreover, there are statements made by members of the Australian team, and other Pakistani players like Rashid Latif. In my opinion, after I have left cricket, there has been match-fixing and betting. When I was working, Intikhab Alam was manager and I always found him to be a decent person. If he has stated that there has been match-fixing, he should be believed.

In '94, when allegations of match-fixing surfaced, I went to the board which, at that time, was headed by Arif Abassi and told him in the presence of Javed Burki that stern action should be taken against the culprits even though other players might subsequently lose matches. In my opinion, expediency came into the way of the administrators in imposing some punishment as, at that time, the Pakistan team was very strong and they did not want to disrupt it. Stern action must be taken against the culprits to save Pakistan cricket, including bans for life and fines. Ata-ur-Rehman told me that he was paid money by Akram to bowl badly. This was during the last one-day international in New Zealand. Mudassar Nazar, too, told me that other players had informed him that they had indulged in betting in two-three matches.

To date, eighteen players have been penalised after being indicted of wrongdoing or for complicity in some form or the other. The punishments range from life bans to fines. In certain cases, a prolonged hobnobbing with bookmakers was taken to be evidence enough to nail the cricketer in question.

The players thus booked include: Hansie Cronje (South Africa), Salim Malik and Ata-ur-Rehman (Pakistan), Mohammed Azharuddin and Ajay Sharma (India), all of whom were banned for life; Ajay Jadeja, Manoj Prabhakar and team physiotherapist, Ali Irani (India), who were suspended for five years; Herschelle Gibbs and Henry Williams (South Africa), who were suspended for six months and fined; Mark Waugh and Shane Warne (Australia), Wasim Akram, Mushtaq Ahmed, Waqar Younis, Saeed Anwar, Inzamam-ul-Haq and Akram Raza (Pakistan), who were all fined.

However, most of the conclusions that were drawn rested on the depositions and statements of the accused. And an accused seldom tells the complete truth. Caught red-handed, I suspect some of them cooked up stories that exonerated them to whatever extent possible. The fact is, match-fixing still remains a largely unsolved puzzle. Many believe that some of the biggest culprits were the administrators of the game, who knew all about the practice and without whose tacit backing it would not have existed.

And of course, there is the involvement of umpires. Trust me, no cricketer can influence a match as much as an umpire can. It is all about a couple of LBW decisions or those thin edges that go past the batsmen. Umpires can, and have, altered the outcome of the game in many cases and, at least, one international umpire has in the past been indicted for his involvement in match-fixing.

In the last few years, the WCC has put laws in place to curb the practice. Whether that has succeeded in getting rid of this malaise is anybody's guess. But as of today, to the best of my knowledge, fixing a match is difficult. In today's competitive arena, if a cricketer still chooses to under-perform, he does it at the risk of being dropped. Betting in cricket, however, has grown manifold. There are bets being accepted even over which two players would field in the deep in the first fifteen overs of an ODI. Bets are accepted over the composition of the side, who will open the innings, how many wides will be bowled by a bowler, whether a batsman will score a half century in less than fifty balls or more. A cricketer's complicity with bookies in providing information on the above accounts is often referred to as 'spot fixing'.

I had, at one stage, become suspicious of one of our new pacers, Sameer Patel, who despite taking wickets was giving away at least five no-balls in every match. Thereafter, along with Aslam, who I trust implicitly and who, as a keeper, was in the best position to keep a tab on the bowling pattern, I closely monitored the bowling and batting of those players who spent a lot of time on their cellphones and who had more than usual number of visitors. Fortunately, I did not find anything that would suggest their involvement in these lesser forms of fixing.

The reason why betting is such a menace today is because of the astronomical volume of money involved. The sum total of estimated bets on an ODI involving any of the top eight teams could be anywhere in the vicinity of two hundred crore rupees.

My own brush with a bookie was in South Africa in 1999. It was early in the morning of a match at Durban. I was just about to leave my room when I got an SMS from an unknown number. It read: 'How is the weather outside?' I automatically glanced out of the window – it was a bright, sunny day. Just then, I got another

SMS from the same number: 'Thundershowers have been predicted for afternoon. Ask your captain to field first if he wins the toss.'

At the team meeting the previous night, we had decided to bat first if we won the toss because the Duckworth Lewis method, put into place if a match is interrupted by weather, is tilted heavily in favour of the side batting first. I was sure, therefore, that the text was from a bookie who had bet on India losing.

I couldn't be bothered dealing with this on the day of a game, so I simply switched my phone off. We lost the match anyway, but later that evening, I was surprised when Vinay told me that he had received an identical SMS. We reported the matter to the team manager and since we hadn't responded to the messages, we didn't get any more of them.

In 2003, Baljeet told me that he had been approached by a bookmaker in a very strange way in the West Indies. He was relaxing in the hotel pool when an attractive girl swam up to him and told him that the West Indian batsman, Roberts, wanted to discuss with him something important. She offered to accompany Baljeet to Roberts' room right away. Baljeet, unsure about what was going on, went with her to Roberts' room.

After the customary exchange of courtesies, the girl left. Roberts then spelt out his agenda rather brazenly. 'Our pride is at stake tomorrow. We just can't lose this match. You are the key bowler for India. I want you to bowl badly.' Baljeet was asked to bowl wide off the stumps. He was promised two hundred thousand US dollars – delivered to his room in the next half hour – if he agreed. Baljeet had stalked out of the room, roundly cursing Roberts in Punjabi.

Baljeet told me about this incident much later when I became captain. I asked him why he hadn't reported the matter to the team management. He said he had, but they had chosen to look the other way.

Then, two years ago, during a series against Pakistan, a rather obsessive fan seemed to be following Aslam everywhere. The fan was his late 30s or early 40s, and always wore dark glasses. He called himself Bobby, stayed in the same hotel as we did, sang endless praises of Aslam, and tried to get friendly with other members of the side as well. One evening, over a drink at a small gathering in the hotel restaurant, Bobby asked Aslam, 'How much do you earn playing?' Aslam was taken aback by the directness of this query. Before he could react, Bobby added, 'There is a way by which you can right away get an amount you would make only after playing for ten years.' Aslam asked Bobby what this was, but Bobby would not reveal anything. He only said that Aslam would first have to say yes to him. Aslam, his suspicions awakened, immediately left the place.

Aslam told me what had happened. We decided to meet Bobby in his room that night. We had decided that we would play along and make Bobby divulge whatever was on his mind. I knew I was taking a big risk by doing this, but I wanted to find out who was paying Bobby to do this. To our shock, Bobby had already checked out by then.

We never saw Bobby again. Eight months after the incident, the Delhi police arrested a bookmaker on suspicion of fixing the final of a recent tri-series – it turned out to be Bobby.

I have often tried to understand why a player would succumb to being bribed. Greed is obviously the most plausible cause, aided by the uncertainties inherent in the career of an international cricketer.

The other reason that people cite is fear of the underworld. But cricket betting has existed much before the underworld stepped into the lucrative arena. And it was only when certain cricketers started double-crossing bookies that the latter took recourse to the underworld. By that time, these cricketers were so entangled, that the underworld only ensured that there was no way out for them.

But the underworld, by and large, holds no threat to a 'clean' cricketer. If it did, then Vinay, Baljeet, Aslam and I wouldn't feel safe. We do though, and still play to win.

When we lost against Kenya in the World Cup, all sorts of conspiracy theories floated in the air. It was hinted that we had thrown away the game because of some underhanded deal. The allegations were baseless, of course.

Interestingly, the betting stakes are the maximum in a match between a top team and a much lower ranked team. Let me elucidate this with an example. Let's say that in the match against Kenya, the *satta*, or betting rates, on India winning was about 25 paise to the rupee, whereas on Kenya winning it was 800 paise to the rupee. So, a person betting a thousand rupees on India winning would make ₹1,250 if India won. However, a person putting a thousand rupees on Kenya winning would make eight thousand rupees if that team won. It's obvious how much more profitable betting on a Kenya win is, notwithstanding its low probability. Now, this is where bookmakers are likely to fix matches and try and ensure that the less fancied team wins.

But while their tactics may have worked in the past, the thought of an Indian cricketer throwing away the World Cup for monetary benefits is indigestible to me. Agreed, Vinay batted a lot more slowly than he should have; Ishan did bowl a wayward line; Amod got out to a poor shot; and I was run out stealing an extra single that wasn't there. But it was just a bad day in office: it was sheer bad luck that this bad day came at such an inopportune moment.

There have been murmurs of our involvement in betting and match-fixing on other occasions as well. For instance, three years ago, the then captain Amod chose to bat first on a green top at Mohali, when it had been decided in the dressing room that, should we win the toss, we would field first. We were bowled out for a paltry 187 and West Indies won the match. Till date, Amod does not have a satisfactory reason as to why he changed his mind and opted to bat first. All he said was that it was his gut feeling that our batsmen would come good.

I remember yet another peculiar incident that took place nearly five years ago. Despite attaining a lead of nearly 350 runs in the first innings, on a spinning track at Nagpur, our then coach, the ex-Indian batsman Shishir Doshi, remained adamant about not imposing a follow-on. The result: we drew a match that was virtually impossible not to win. Shishir was subsequently removed as coach amidst speculation about his friendship with some fishy characters.

There have been two occasions when players backed out on the eve of crucial matches, citing injuries. For instance, Ramgopal pulled out of our World Cup game against West Indies, citing an old ankle injury. Obviously, the absence of an in-form bowler impacts the team in a big way. For us, it was bound to be even more demoralising as we had already lost our main strike bowler, Ishan. This meant that we had to enter a do-or-die match with a crippled bowling attack.

Just a day prior to the match, Ramgopal had seemed fine in the nets. He bowled a good line and the rhythm was just superb. Of course, it is possible that his old injury started acting up later, but given the stakes involved, there was bound to be speculation. One reassuring factor, though, is that a player is declared unfit to play only after a thorough assessment by the team physiotherapist. And I'm sure our Australian physio, Daniel, who has been with us for the last two years, would never be dishonest.

◆

16

RETIRED HURT!

So that had been the content of my report. I had indicted at least six players of serious irresponsibility: Ishan had been party to technical corruption and taken drugs, as had Jeet; Shreyas and Amod had put monetary interests above team interests at least at some point; Jeet, Baljeet and Rajat were guilty of indiscipline on the eve of matches.

When I'd finished the report, although I was still deeply disappointed about the World Cup defeat, I wasn't sure whether I was going to actually submit it to the board. For all my apprehensions about the colleagues I was indicting, I felt strongly that I should go ahead with it. And that this report was a year too late.

I read the report again on my way to Kolkata where the meeting of the Action Committee was taking place. I wondered whether I would have reported all these incidents in any other situation. Agreed, Sunil Kapoor had asked for an honest report, and I had prepared one; but had my negative state of mind clouded my judgement? After all, I had known about the drugs, the womanising, the greed all along. But these were men who were great players and to attribute our loss at the World Cup to their vices was an escapist way of looking at things. And if there was one thing I was not, it was an escapist.

When I was in school and struggling even to keep my place in the school side, my father had once tapped me on my shoulder and said, in a well-meaning way, 'The easiest thing for you to do is concentrate on studies.' I knew my father did not believe in my abilities in cricket. What he said remained with me for a long time. Then, as much as now, if I'm given two options, I'll always go for the one I believe in, regardless of whether it is less trodden or more difficult. Why then was I going ahead with this report, which *was*, perhaps, the easier way out for me?

Simultaneously, a conflicting thought floated in my mind. The report might be able to set things right – I was merely carrying out a responsibility. Of course, everyone is entitled to their share of idiosyncrasies, but as captain, I had to take a call on whether a player, with all his failings – cricketing or otherwise – was still useful to the team or not. Doing so badly at the World Cup was, perhaps, impetus enough for me to visit these dark alleys.

As I reached Kolkata, I felt more inclined to stick to the report's 'no-holds-barred' content. I didn't care if it shook the world of cricket; I didn't care if it won me enemies overnight. Nothing could be worse than the way we had lost those matches at the World Cup.

I was prepared to face and fight another day.

✦

It was 8.30 in the evening by the time I got back home. As I walked into our house, I saw my parents and Revathi sitting in the living room. Dad had an eye on the news channel playing in the background.

I went to mom and asked about her health and then turned to my father. Seeing his tense expression, I asked, 'What happened, Dad?'

He gestured towards the television and increased the volume. A correspondent was reporting, 'Indian skipper Mayank Pradhan, today, reportedly offered to resign from captaincy. The cricket board has rejected the offer. In Kolkata to attend the Action Committee meeting, Pradhan took full responsibility for India's dismal showing in the World Cup. He refused to blame any individual, instead attributing India's performance to a 'lack of application on the part of senior batsmen, clumsy fielding and wayward bowling'. Pradhan is reported to have told the board that India's dismal performance could have no quick-fix solution. Instead, he suggested a complete overhaul of the domestic and junior-level cricket structures to better groom players for the future. Pradhan has been named captain for the series against Sri Lanka.'

Dad looked at me, full of questions I had no answers to. What I had said at the Action Committee meeting was something I had thought about on my way from the Kolkata airport to the Taj Bengal Hotel. Had I chickened out? I did not know.

I looked at my father again; I could see he was unhappy, even a little annoyed that I had offered myself as the sacrificial lamb. I knew there wouldn't be much conversation that night. I turned towards my room.

'Shall we have dinner?' Mom asked.

'No, I'm not hungry.'

Dad got up and patted my shoulder. I could sense that, while he was trying to convey that he still supported me, it was because he was my father and I his son; it wasn't for the merit of what I had done. At that moment, I did not feel brave enough to turn and face dad. I retreated to my room.

That night, Revathi and I had a heated argument; it had been many years since our last one.

'What is it, Mayank, that you can't share with me? Why have you been behaving so strangely all evening?'

I had never felt so helpless in all my life. I stayed silent, but Revathi isn't one to let go that easily.

'Listen Mayank, you have shared everything with me. What is it about this report that makes you so tense? Why did you take all the blame on yourself? Why did you throw away this opportunity to tell the board about the players responsible for the defeat? Tell me, Mayank.'

'What did you expect me to do, Revathi?' I shouted back, surprising Revathi as much as myself. 'I mean,' I said, consciously lowering my voice, 'what option did I have? There are so many factors that were responsible for our defeat, most of which have accumulated over the years and which I was privy to. Had I been man enough, I would have addressed these issues before the World Cup; and if it were beyond my powers to do so, I ought to have resigned the captaincy then. With what face could I report those issues now?'

Revathi looked confounded by my outburst. She said, 'I want to read the report.'

I handed it to her, and she started reading it. I sat still while she went through it, my mind occupied with other things.

It took Revathi an hour to complete the report. When she turned the last page she looked at me, her eyes full of sympathy.

I couldn't hold back my emotions. In a choked voice, I said, 'I wanted to give up the captaincy today.'

She nodded understandingly. I reached out and took her hand in mine as I continued, 'But I'm glad my offer was rejected. I want to redeem myself for this defeat. And I want to do so with the key members of this team in it. That will be the ultimate test of my leadership and character. And I want to pass that test before hanging up my boots.'

Revathi hugged me hard as I broke down and cried.

24 June 2008

It's 10.10 p.m. The entire team is dining together. I put up a brave front, crack a couple of jokes and generally try to keep the mood buoyant. Deep down, I'm still nervous. In just twenty-four hours from now, we'll know if we are the world champions or not. We'll know whether 25 June can be lucky twice over for us or not.

Later, I speak to Revathi at length and feel better. She would have been here with me, had her father not been ill. After I hang up, I start flipping through news channels, all of which seem to be carrying previews of our match. I know I need to sleep early and sleep well tonight. As I'm preparing to hit the sack, a thought occurs to me – perhaps I should confide in Vinay; perhaps, I should tell him about the alleged involvement of three of our players in having fixed tomorrow's final. After all, if there is someone whose credibility has never been doubted it is Vinay.

Ten minutes later, I'm in Vinay's room. He looks disturbed, but not shocked, when I tell him about the allegations. 'Nearly four years ago, a journalist told me that a bookmaker had offered him two million rupees if he would introduce the bookmaker to me. I had asked the journalist to report the matter to the police, but I don't know if he did,' Vinay tells me.

This information compounds my fears. I have suspected that bookmakers, via journalists or otherwise, have had an access to my players for quite some time. While I trust Vinay implicitly, I can't say the same about others.

Another half hour has gone by. Vinay and I are still deliberating over the matter. One option that comes to my mind is to hold a press conference the next morning and tell the world what I've come to know. If I know Tiwari well, he wouldn't mind being dragged into the controversy. Such a step would alert authorities and make them take a microscopic view of every ball sent down in the match. Thus, assuming that three of our players have actually decided to under-perform, the knowledge that they are being closely watched will make them change their mind.

On the flip side, the announcement might just spread panic in the cricket world and all our cricketers would be under undue pressure on the eve of this crucial match. This is when Vinay comes up with an idea, which I buy: I never knew Vinay and Imran Khan thought alike!

◆

17

LORD'S

25 June 2008

It is a clear and sunny day; a mild breeze is blowing. The match is about to start in another thirty-five minutes. It is probably the biggest match in all our careers – none of us has been in the finals of a World Cup before.

It's a strange situation in the dressing room, however. There is no last-minute strategising happening. Instead, each of the members of the selected eleven has put one hand on the national tricolour. The mood is tense. I make them swear that they will give their best to the country and go all out to win; that they will not under-perform and throw away the match.

I win the toss and decide to bat first. This surprises commentators who believe that the ball will seam early on. Sharath Jaidev, interviewing me on TV, asks me why am I choosing to bat first. I tell him that it's been my mantra always to bat first in a crucial match and put up an imposing, intimidating total.

I walk back into the dressing room after the toss. The match will start in fifteen minutes. Asad and Amod are padding up. Amod looks a bit tense and that's understandable because, in all probability, it is his last World Cup match and he'd like to win it for us. I look at Vinay. He gives me a reassuring look, implying that all seems well and that the match-fixing rumour was, in all likelihood, a hoax. I hope that's true.

I have a word with Amod and Asad. I tell them to be cautious in the first six overs, which is when the fielding restrictions are on. They must play themselves in first and play the ball on merit. Asad nods. Amod looks uncharacteristically lost. I know there is something on his mind; I get a feeling it's not the game. He looks into my eyes and blurts out: 'The day before yesterday, a former Indian cricketer offered me two crore rupees to throw away this match.'

'What?' I say, unable to register the meaning of his words.

Amod repeats what he has just said.

'Who? Sharath Jaidev?' I've never liked Sharath.

'No.'

There's a deafening pause. In this one moment, before Amod says the cricketer's name, a hundred names flash through my mind.

'Vinod Bhargava,' he says. 'He met me after the team dinner two days ago. He said I should take an off-stump guard in the final match, since the Australians tend to bowl to me on my legs. The off-stump guard would have put me in inconvenience and, thus, would have made me more susceptible to falling LBW. He told me how much I would be paid, and then said another member of the side had already accepted the offer.'

'So what did you do?'

'I asked him to fuck off.'

'And he did?'

'Yes, but he was so brazen, I felt sure he has been into this for a long time. And not just that, possibly he has people in the side with him.'

As I hear this, I feel my faith being shattered. I think of my recent interactions with Vinod and see designs everywhere. Suddenly, a thought strikes me: Why was he so keen that Naved not play in the final?

'Do you have any idea who the other player is, who accepted the offer?' I ask.

'No. But Vinod did mention in passing that he is a bowler.'

I feel a strong sense of panic. We're going into the match with three pacers and a solitary spinner. It can't be Naved; which means it has to be one or possibly more among Rajat, Ishan and Baljeet.

'That bastard did come to me,' Rajat suddenly blurts from behind. 'He started by telling me that I should bowl a little short, as my good length bowls tended to get over-pitched and were easy to drive. I told him the Australians were good at playing the pull short. He told me they wouldn't against me, as they weren't used to me pitching the ball short. When I didn't seem convinced, he told me I would get paid ₹1.5 crore if I did what he asked.'

'And what did you tell him?'

'That I'd think about it and let him know.'

'What?' I ask him in shock. Rajat becomes aware of the looks he is getting from everybody. 'Look,' he says aggressively, 'I had to tell him that because I was scared for my life. I have heard about the kind of clout that bookmakers enjoy in the underworld. I was dead scared. But I immediately switched off my cell so that Vinod couldn't get across to me. And even when he came to the ground during yesterday's practice, I avoided him.'

'But why the hell didn't you both tell me what was going on?'

Amod speaks up, 'I didn't because I thought Vinod and you were very close.'

'So?' I ask.

'Well, you never know who is what over here,' explains Rajat. 'There was a slight suspicion in my mind that you too could be involved, especially as you were the one who had invited Vinod for the team dinner that night,' he says.

I don't understand what's happening around me; suddenly I'm the one being looked at with suspicion. We have just two minutes before the start of the match. The mood couldn't be more damaging before a match as crucial as this. At this point, Vinay takes charge, like a senior pro, 'Listen guys, the match is going to start soon. You've got to put everything behind and just concentrate on the game. Okay?'

I know it's not okay. Yet, I'm too perplexed to have a definite idea about anything.

Amod and Asad are now at the crease. Amod is taking guard. No, he isn't taking an off-stump guard for sure. I sit in the players' box and watch. Baljeet comes and sits next to me. 'Bhai,' he says, 'a journalist friend had told me way back after our first match against Kenya in the World Cup that he suspected Vinod was involved in match-fixing. . . .'

I don't want to hear anything more. I know that whatever happens over the next three-and-a-half hours – a wide, a run out, a missed catch – I'm going to view it all with suspicion.

♦

18

HISTORY

INDIA beats Australia to lift World Cup

*'You have to be attacking every moment in this game no matter what,'
said Dave Symonds before this match. India did just that – recovering
from 38 for 4, thanks to some rare big hitting by Jeet and Aslam and
then, throttling Australia to take the four-run victory and win the
World Cup.*

*At one stage, India were in trouble at 46 for 4 after ten overs.
The Indian batsmen seemed afflicted yet again with their 'finals jinx'.
Both Asad and Shreyas fell early to some astute swing bowling by Peter
Marsh, who exploited the breezy conditions to the hilt. Later, Vinay
Bhagat was run out by a direct throw from mid-wicket by Dennis Jones
and Mayank Pradhan miscued a pull shot so that the ball just popped
up high, giving the mid-wicket fielder a simple catch. Jeet Gohil, too,
gifted his wicket away cheaply. But just when the Indian innings seemed
down and out, an unexpected resurgence was to be seen.*

*Amod and Aslam Khan each played a spectacular innings, hammering
the ball left, right and centre, as India smashed 125 off the last eleven*

overs of their innings. It was the speed and strength with which the pair picked up their runs that surprised one and all. Both Amod and Aslam struck four mighty sixes – Jeet targeting John McDermott in particular with three consecutive maximums over midwicket.

Baljeet Gujral, who had had a great semi-final match, also played his part when it mattered, by removing Dennis Jones for 24 to break a powerful opening stand of 62 with Darren Moody, who made 50. With Australia still cruising, Baljeet then hooked Australia's big fish, Kevin Symonds. The master of flash, Symonds tried one improvisation too far and was bowled through his legs, trying to reverse-sweep a quicker dart. Peter Hogg fell in the same over, run-out in a mix-up with Greg Matt for 1, and again the momentum switched back to India.

Later, in the penultimate over, with Australia needing 21 from twelve balls, the experienced Ishan Sawant took two wickets and there was a further run-out as the pressure told on Australia. Ishan finished with a credible 2 for 20 from four overs, and Australia came up short – despite Peter Marsh's fiery efforts. When he holed out on the cover boundary for 28 off Rajat Shetty's last ball, Australia's hopes fell away.

India's victory here at Lord's holds huge historical significance. It was at this venue and on this date that India won the ODI World cup exactly twenty-five years ago. That destiny should have planned this triumph today, with such minute attention to detail, is indeed a remarkable and the most memorable facet of this win. One hopes that this win inspires a new generation of Indian cricketers, much as the '83 win did.

India 166 for 8 (Amod Roy 57, Aslam Khan 42) off 20 overs beat **Australia** 162 for 8 off 20 overs (Darren Moody 50, Ishan Sawant 2-20) by four runs.

✦

As the whole stadium erupts in joy, I feel numb. We've done it. We are the Twenty20 world champions. We've beaten Australia by a mere four runs. The margin of victory, though, is immaterial. I have always believed in what a friend told me long ago: 'Victories are fragile when you achieve them ... they grow stronger with time.'

I am overwhelmed with a sense of fulfilment I have never experienced before. When four of our players hug me simultaneously, my chest feels strained, I think I might just have a heart attack. I am breathless. And then, as we all run a victory lap around the stadium holding the tricolour in our hands, I realise that I have never felt prouder. Not when I first donned the India cap, not when I scored my first century, not when I first helped India win a match.

As I hold the coveted trophy, my hands tremble somewhat with the sheer weight of it. After all, twelve world-class teams have competed for it; several million worshippers of the game have aspired to see their country acquire it. I give a speech that is incoherent; sheer ecstasy has got the better of me as I bask in this cricketing glory.

The only time I have experienced a similar emotion was when I held my son, Ayush, in my arms for the first time. But that was a personal joy; here I am basking in the exhilaration of millions of people.

And then, suddenly, I sense some commotion in the presentation area. Something suddenly seems to have gone amiss. An official walks up to the announcer, Irfan Raza, and talks to him. Irfan's expression changes from curiosity to shock.

Raza then makes the announcement: 'Ladies and gentlemen, it is with profound grief that I have to tell you that former Indian cricketer Vinod Bhargava is no more. He was found dead in his hotel room while the match was on.'

From frenzied excitement, numbness envelops the whole stadium.

I was supposed to attend a press conference immediately after the presentation. I'm not sure if I'm prepared for it now. In another fifteen minutes, I'm facing the scribes. Most of the queries revolve around Vinod's death. A rather bizarre theory doing the rounds is that three Indian players were expected to throw the match; when this didn't happen, Vinod killed himself because he was now in trouble with the bigger bookies.

'The theory doesn't deserve a comment from me,' is what I say. I know I sound rude, but I don't care.

Later I'm told that a report had appeared in an Indian daily that morning, accusing Vinod of being a bookmaker. Tiwari had penned the report. The report hints that he had bribed two cricketers in our team to lose the match, but does not divulge their names. We don't know yet if it was suicide, murder, or a natural death. I wonder if we'll ever really know.

An hour later, we are finally back at the hotel. There is total chaos. Security has been increased manifold, which means that each cricketer is escorted from the hotel portico to the lobby by some half a dozen security personnel. Scribes try their best to extract sound bites from us, but fail.

At the seventh floor dining hall, where we all eventually assemble, confusion prevails. We are told that a police team will be coming to question us so we must all stay in the hotel. Half an hour later, the police team arrives. Each of the team members is then questioned one by one. The interrogation goes on for anywhere between ten minutes to an hour. After each cricketer is done with his interrogation, he is allowed to do whatever he wants to for the rest of the evening. The players are feeling low despite the win. Jeet, Aslam, Rajat and Amod head to the bar for a drink; the others simply retreat to the confines of their rooms.

My interrogation is the longest – perhaps because of the general perception that I've been close to Vinod. By the end of it, I'm mentally dead. Our win at Lord's already seems to belong to a different life.

19

KEENAN STADIUM, JAMSHEDPUR

30 June 2008

Five days have passed since our World Cup win. Our victory has slightly upstaged the shock over Vinod's death because, thanks to Tiwari's report, a perception seems to have formed that Vinod was, indeed, a bookmaker. The police remain tight-lipped on the issue; that investigations are on is all they are willing to say.

It is noon. I am at the Keenan Stadium for a special felicitation by the Jharkhand Cricket Council. Along with the council's top officials and all the players representing Jharkhand in different tournaments, also present is the MD of Tata Steel. The local MP is expected to join us any moment. I can see another familiar face – Father Joe Fernandes, principal of my alma mater. Revathi was supposed to be with me, but a court hearing in the morning means that she will join my parents and son at the special VVIP enclosure, adjoining my dais, later.

I have been feeling a bit jaded by the unending felicitations. It is getting monotonous and I hate this feeling of boredom. But

Jharkhand is my home team after all, and I am particularly fond of the Keenan Stadium. A crowd of some twenty-five thousand people has assembled, this time exclusively for me. Many of these people I'm sure must be familiar to me – some of them would have come and seen me play at this venue; others may have gathered outside my house or at the railway station every time I returned from a successful series. I wouldn't recognise them though. That doesn't, however, diminish our mutual sense of belonging.

I think about what I'm going to announce soon, and the shock it will be for people. I think about the huge excited crowd that has assembled only to share my happiness. I'm not sure if everyone will be as happy by the time the function ends.

The MP finally makes his way in. I see Revathi rush in just as the function is about to start. I feel reassured. Regardless of how anyone at the stadium reacts, I know Revathi will stand by me.

The felicitation progresses in much the same way as similar other functions have. The local MP garlands me and confers upon me the honour of 'Jamshedpur Ratna'. In my speech, I thank as many people as profoundly as I can for all their wishes and love. And then, I begin with the hardest part.

'I take this opportunity to make a special announcement here. It has been a tremendous privilege to play for the country for the last eleven years and to lead the side in the last three. I do, however, feel that the biggest leadership challenge is to identify the right time to let a younger lot take over. That is how you can ensure consistent, continued excellence. I do feel that, with the Twenty20 World Cup victory behind us, the confidence level of our players is at its peak. This is the next generation, the future of our cricket for the next ten years.'

I can feel a deafening silence engulf the ground. Everybody seems to guess what I am going to say next. I glance at Revathi. I know she's not too happy with my decision, but there's a reassuring smile on her face.

'I would, thus, be glad to hand over charge to a younger leader. I'd like to announce my retirement from ODIs and Twenty20 matches. Henceforth, I'll only be available for Test matches and serve the team as best I can. Once again, thank you all so much.'

There is a buzz around the stadium, and on the dais. Nobody quite knows how to react. I'm convinced about what I've done, though. The World Cup win had breathed new life into our cricket; the team was ready for a new beginning, and it was only appropriate that this new beginning was made under a new leader.

The day is not yet over. Journalists who were, in any case, scheduled to have a session with me, now have more to ask after my announcement.

'Does your timing have something to do with Vinod Bhargava's death?'

'No,' I answer calmly.

'Do you think your decision might be seen as selfish; a decision taken because you want to be seen as quitting when you're on top?' a young journalist from a news channel asks me.

'I don't make my decisions based on what people might think.'

My answer is terse, but adequate I think. Then I'm struck by a feeling of remorse; perhaps, I owed a better explanation to the thousands of people who've supported me through my career. 'Every achiever, in my opinion, blocks the emergence of other achievers and talented professionals if he clings to his throne longer than he should. And this is true not just in sports, but across all fields. India is a young country. She deserves younger and more dynamic politicians, business leaders and sportspersons. In life, your roles change with age. So does it need to be in cricket and elsewhere.

'Besides, in every career, there is one cherished dream that spurs you on and keeps you hungry and focussed. Mine was to win the World Cup for my country. Now that it has been accomplished, I'm not sure whether I'll be able to retain the same motivation and zest. It makes sense, then, to hand over the mantle to someone who is still greedy for victory.

'I've always believed that in life there are no facts, only interpretations. Thus, I leave it to all of you to decide whether I am being selfish or selfless.'

At the end of my speech, people stand up and clap. To be really honest, I have had some doubts about whether my supporters would stand by my decision. But these doubts evaporate in the face of the applause that my speech receives. The expressions on Revathi's and my parents' faces bear the same happiness that I have seen on them after some of my more cherished achievements.

✦

The next morning I wake up early. Something in me propels me to head for my alma mater, Loyola School. It is a Saturday and the school is largely empty.

I head for the cricket field. I'm glad to see a bunch of young boys practising despite the cloudy weather. They crowd around me first, and then, I start helping them in their practice, giving them tips, pointing out flaws. I'm surprised at how quickly two hours pass.

I think, at a subconscious level, I already have a mission on my mind. I want to identify the next big talent who can make a mark at the international level. After all, my eleven years in international cricket have proved that quality cricket in India is no longer the domain of big town boys.

A fourteen-year-old boy is getting ready to bowl to me. In all my growing years, I was clear about the cricketers I idolised and wanted to emulate – the ones whose talent inspired me to play for the country. I think I would be disappointed if I did not, in turn, serve as an inspiration to someone. As I take guard, I think about how that would truly make my journey as a cricketer, as also the larger journey of life, worth everything.

◆